About Island Press

Island Press is the only nonprofit organization in the United States whose principal purpose is the publication of books on environmental issues and natural resource management. We provide solutions-oriented information to professionals, public officials, business and community leaders, and concerned citizens who are shaping responses to environmental problems.

In 2000, Island Press celebrates its sixteenth anniversary as the leading provider of timely and practical books that take a multidisciplinary approach to critical environmental concerns. Our growing list of titles reflects our commitment to bringing the best of an expanding body of literature to the environmental community throughout North America and the world.

Support for Island Press is provided by The Jenifer Altman Foundation, The Bullitt Foundation, The Mary Flagler Cary Charitable Trust, The Nathan Cummings Foundation, The Geraldine R. Dodge Foundation, The Charles Engelhard Foundation, The Ford Foundation, The German Marshall Fund of the United States, The George Gund Foundation, The Vira I. Heinz Endowment, The William and Flora Hewlett Foundation, The W. Alton Jones Foundation, The John D. and Catherine T. MacArthur Foundation, The Andrew W. Mellon Foundation, The Charles Stewart Mott Foundation, The Curtis and Edith Munson Foundation, The National Fish and Wildlife Foundation, The New-Land Foundation, The Oak Foundation, The Overbrook Foundation, The David and Lucile Packard Foundation, The Pew Charitable Trusts, The Rockefeller Brothers Fund, Rockefeller Financial Services, The Winslow Foundation, and individual donors.

Planning for a New Century

Planning for a New Century

the regional agenda

edited by **jonathan barnett**

ISLAND PRESS
Washington, D.C. • Covelo, California

Library of Congress Cataloging-in-Publication Data

Planning for a new century : the regional agenda / edited by Jonathan Barnett ; foreword by David Rusk ; essays by Jonathan Barnett ... [et al.].
   p. cm.
Includes bibliographical references and index.
  ISBN 1-55963-806-0 (acid-free)
  1. Regional planning—United States. 2. Economic development—Environmental aspects—United States. 3. Public welfare—United States. I. Barnett, Jonathan.
  HT392 .P547 2001
  307.1'2'0973—dc21

                                    00-011162

Contents

Foreword by David Rusk   ix

Editor's Note   xiv

Introduction: An Agenda for the New Century   1
Jonathan Barnett

Part 1: The New Metropolitanism

CHAPTER 1. Regional Imperatives of Global Competition   11
Theodore Hershberg

CHAPTER 2. Planning Metropolitan Regions   31
Gary Hack

Part 2: Managing Growth and Conserving the Environment

CHAPTER 3. Social Equity and Metropolitan Growth   49
John C. Keene

CHAPTER 4. Regional Design: Local Codes as Cause and Cure of Sprawl   63
Jonathan Barnett

CHAPTER 5. Next Steps in Controlling Pollution   77
Roger Raufer

CHAPTER 6. Highway Planning and Land Use: Theory and Practice   89
Stephen H. Putman

Part 3: Education, Safety, and Welfare

CHAPTER 7. Improving Primary and Secondary Education   105
Susan H. Fuhrman

CHAPTER 8. Improving Public Safety in Cities   119
Thomas M. Seamon

CHAPTER 9. Welfare Reform, Reproductive Reform, or Work Reform?   131
Roberta Rehner Iversen

Part 4: Restoring Older Urban Areas

CHAPTER 10. Housing and Urban Communities   149
Eugenie L. Birch

CHAPTER 11. Restoring Natural Resources and Rebuilding Urban Communities   165
Anne Whiston Spirn

CHAPTER 12. Downtowns: Competitive for a New Century   177
Paul R. Levy

Afterword by Judith Rodin   195

Suggestions for Further Reading   199

About the Contributors   203

Index   209

Foreword

David Rusk

America has become a metropolitan nation.

A century ago almost two-thirds of the population lived in rural areas. Only 22 percent lived in communities with more than 50,000 residents, and the notion of metropolitan regions had yet to be conceived. Four out of ten people worked on farms, producing a quarter of the nation's output.

Today 80 percent of our population lives in 277 metropolitan areas, which account for 85 percent of the national economy. The number of farmers has shrunk from 40 percent of all workers to less than 3 percent, and agriculture contributes only 2 percent to the gross domestic product. We have two million more schoolteachers and college professors than farmworkers.

America's future thus depends on the health and vitality of our metro areas.

In 1999, Fannie Mae polled experts about the factors that have shaped urban America over the past fifty years. The top ten influences were the Federal-Aid Highway Act of 1956 and the dominance of the automobile, FHA mortgage financing and subdivision regulation, the deindustrialization of central cities, urban renewal, in the form of downtown redevelopment and public housing projects, mass production of suburban tract housing, as in the case of Levittown, racial segregation and job discrimination in cities and suburbs, enclosed shopping malls, Sunbelt-style sprawl, air-conditioning, and the urban riots of the 1960s.

The experts were also asked to project what the ten major factors shaping urban America over the next fifty years will be. Their list consisted of growing disparities in wealth, the suburban political majority, the aging of the baby boomers, the perpetual underclass in central cities and inner suburbs, smart-growth initiatives to limit sprawl, the Internet, deterioration of the "first ring" post-1945 suburbs, shrinking household size, the expanded system of "outer beltways" to serve new edge cities, and racial integration reflecting the increasing diversity of cities and suburbs.

There is a curious dichotomy between the two lists. Public policies—what I call "the rules of the game"—dominate the first list. Most notable are the Federal-Aid Highway Act of 1956, FHA mortgage financing, and urban renewal. In hindsight, we can also see how public policies created the conditions for other major influences on metropolitan growth: deindustrialization, suburban tract housing, segregation, shopping malls, sprawl, even urban riots. Only the advent of air-conditioning was independent of public policy.

But most of the experts' list of influences on the next fifty years seems disengaged from any public-policy context. Growing disparities of wealth, the aging of baby boomers, the perpetual urban underclass, the deterioration of "first ring" suburbs, and shrinking household size all have an aura of inevitable demographic trends or immutable realities of the supposed "free market." Only two future factors—smart-growth initiatives and outer beltways—are clearly grounded in the public policy environment.

Have we entered a new era of so-called free market determinism? I doubt it. It is hard to think of another sector of our economy more shaped by public policy and more dependent on public investment than land development. What the second list reflects, I believe, is the experts' implicit expectation that future metropolitan trends will be shaped by today's rules of the game.

Playing by today's rules is not the perspective of the authors of *Planning for a New Century: The Regional Agenda.* The book's editor, Jonathan Barnett, and the eleven contributors knowledgeably cover a wide range of topics, such as transportation and land-use planning, zoning and design, housing, public education, welfare reform, public safety, downtown revitalization, pollution control, and protection of open spaces and natural areas. Many chapters end with specific policy recommendations, and most are framed in a metropolitan-wide or regional context—a sharp break from the city-only focus of the past. Viewed as a whole, the recommendations would substantially transform metropolitan America for the better.

Yet an almost unseen presence hovers over most of the topics, perhaps just fleetingly glimpsed, like noiseless flashes of heat lightning over the horizon on a hot summer day. That pervasive presence is an invisible man—quite literally, it is black novelist Ralph Ellison's *Invisible Man*. It is the issue of race.

Race is certainly not ignored in this book, yet the issue deserves to be highlighted even more. The evidence shows very compellingly that two factors—sprawl and race—have shaped American metropolitan areas' evolution over the past five decades. Sprawl and race are interrelated. They interact with each other. They are linked most clearly through the concentration of poverty that is itself a racially shaped urban phenomenon.

Why are sprawl and race intertwined? Let me describe a sequence of cause and effect. Most young, middle-class family heads say their primary reasons for choosing where they live are good schools and safe neighborhoods. Other factors—the house's physical qualities or investment potential, the commute to work, and the like—fall further down on the list. (Incidentally, the level of local taxes paid and the quality of local public services typically bring up the bottom of the list, if they are mentioned at all.)

Middle-class families are clearly shunning (or sometimes actually fleeing) purportedly poor schools and dangerous neighborhoods. Yet what most parents consider "poor schools" do not typically reflect their evaluation of the quality of principals, teachers, curricula, or facilities. "Poor schools" are deemed "poor" because invariably they have a lot of poor children in them. Similarly, almost all high-crime neighborhoods have high concentrations of poor people.

Concentrated poverty creates "push" factors—poor schools, high crime, neighborhood deterioration, falling property values, and often both high tax rates and declining public services—that push middle-class families out of high-poverty city neighborhoods. Conversely, newer suburbs are exerting "pull" factors—good schools, safer neighborhoods, rising home values, better local services, and often lower tax rates—that pull middle-class families into them.

The attractive attributes of newer suburbs are not the result of some superior civic virtue but of the fact that these are low-poverty communities. In fact, as the chapters that follow often document, each generation of new suburbs was designed to be a low-poverty community by a host of national, state, and local policies. And, by design or default, such policies also consigned many inner-city and now older suburban neighborhoods to be warehouses for the majority of the region's poor.

Push and pull factors are substantially two sides of the same coin—concentrated poverty. But concentrated poverty is a very racially dominated phenomenon. Nationally, there are almost twice as many poor white residents of metropolitan areas as poor black or poor Hispanic residents. Yet poor whites rarely live in poor neighborhoods (which are defined as areas where poverty rates exceed 20 percent). Only one-quarter of poor whites live in poverty-impacted neighborhoods; three-quarters live in working-class or middle-class neighborhoods scattered all over our metropolitan areas. By contrast, one-half of poor Hispanics and three-quarters of poor blacks live in poor neighborhoods in inner cities and inner suburbs.

What does this mean? For one thing, if you are poor and white, the odds are three to one that at your neighborhood school your own children's classmates will be primarily middle class. If you are poor and black, the odds are three to one that your own children will be surrounded by other poor schoolchildren. The socioeconomic backgrounds of a child's family and of a child's classmates are the strongest influences shaping success or failure in school.

It takes a school, a neighborhood, and a family to raise and educate a child successfully. Where families are weak, schools and neighborhoods have to be stronger to compensate. But America works in reverse. We surround children from the weakest families with the weakest neighborhoods and schools.

Housing policy is school policy. In fact, integrating poor households into middle-class communities through mandatory, mixed-income housing policies may be the best school policy . . . and the best anticrime policy . . . and the best welfare-to-work policy . . . and the best fiscal policy.

The convergence of poverty and race create the toughest political problems in America. And yet even the concentration of poverty that appears so menacing and formidable is not an insurmountable barrier. Consider this: in the typical metropolitan area, only five of every one hundred residents are poor and white. Of the 5 percent of the population that is poor and white, almost four out of five are already scattered throughout middle-class communities. They still struggle to raise their children, but their task is made much easier by living within mainstream society. And in a typical metropolitan area, only five of every one hundred residents are poor and black or poor and Hispanic. Yet three to four of those five poor minorities live isolated in high-poverty ghettos and barrios—neighborhoods where opportunity continues to vanish.

Making a place for only four or five new neighbors who are poor out of every one hundred residents is not a horrific prospect for many middle-class communities, and that is all that is required if the issue is to be approached on a metropolitan-wide basis. Opening up our mainstream communities to poor minorities as we generally do for poor whites is the true empowerment zone.

Urban sprawl adversely impacts both our natural and human geography and challenges our ability to create more livable communities. But the primary livability issue for urban America is "Are we going to live together?"

Planning for a New Century: The Regional Agenda helps chart the way.

Editor's Note

This book began as an interdisciplinary seminar at the University of Pennsylvania in the spring of 1999. I recorded the talks by each participant, and the tapes were transcribed by my teaching assistant, Komal Shaikh. The transcripts then became reference material to help the authors compose each chapter. Without Ms. Shaikh's diligence and accuracy as a transcriber, this book would have been much more difficult to produce.

Introduction: An Agenda
for a New Century

Jonathan Barnett

We are living in a time of great prosperity and amazing technological advances, but there are some aspects of the way we live that are clearly going wrong; and that continue to get worse.

Gridlocked streets and highways are symptoms of underlying problems in a society increasingly dependent on automobiles for transportation. As work locations and homes become more dispersed, commuting times are getting longer and more frustrating for many people. Employers locating on the rapidly developing fringes of metropolitan regions are separated from the older cities and towns where the people who most need the jobs can afford to live. More hours are spent driving just to accomplish simple household errands, as shops are no longer concentrated in a few locations but are instead spread out along highways. And, of course, people who can't afford a car, or are unable to drive, can't get to these shops, may have more limited job opportunities, and in general feel isolated from the rest of society.

Another symptom of underlying problems is the growing disparity of resources among different areas of the same metropolitan region. Fast growing communities on the metropolitan fringe struggle to pay for schools and infrastructure, established affluent suburbs hold the line on taxes, or even cut them, while many other suburbs and cities struggle to maintain services as the population of people in need grows larger. Cities and towns compete with each other to offer tax subsidies to business and industry, hoping that, in the long run, they will create the tax base they need; but these beggar-your-neighbor policies become self-defeating as more and more communities adopt them, and are truly adverse to older communities that already have weak tax bases.

A third symptom is that irreplaceable farms and forests at the urban fringe are being lost to new development while huge areas of housing and industry in older cities and towns become vacant and virtually abandoned.

The word "sprawl" is often used as shorthand for these kinds of problems. "Sprawl" was originally coined as a pejorative term for seemingly unplanned new development spreading outward from older cities and suburbs, but sprawl also turns out to be the product of a complex interaction among government programs and private enterprise.

Public policies to promote ownership of individual homes, by subsidizing mortgages and making mortgage interest tax deductible, have enabled the housing industry to create a huge improvement in the overall quality of most people's homes. However, the same policies also promoted disinvestment in older urban areas, originally by deliberately excluding older neighborhoods, particularly if they had significant minority populations, and, more recently, by making it comparatively difficult to find funds for renovation and infill development.

The Interstate Highway System is a magnificent achievement, but it was planned to solve existing transportation problems, disregarding the way highways facilitate the migration of industry and commerce to new locations outside of traditional cities and towns, and open up vast new areas for homebuilders. Local governments were often overwhelmed by unexpected growth, while the highways themselves became congested as a result of the development they induced. Highways cut through established urban areas have often proved dysfunctional, destroying neighborhoods and businesses, only to become more impassible than local streets at peak periods of the day.

The adoption of zoning and subdivision codes by most communities was an effective way to take control of their future, but the regulations in these codes—derived from prototypes originally written in the 1920s—have promoted commercial strip development along highways and channeled the production of new houses into subdivisions where all the house lots are the same size—instead of neighborhoods with a variety of house types related to a town or city center.

We are now in the midst of a national conversation about issues like sustainability, smart growth, and livable communities. Knowing that public policies helped create today's problems, it is reasonable to expect that public policies can help correct them.

The issues are remarkably similar almost everywhere in the United States. Differences in regional culture are far less significant than they used to be, as so many people move from one area to another, read the same periodicals, and watch the same movies and television programs. Philadelphia has a very different history from Houston or Los Angeles, but the pattern of development in the three-state Delaware Valley region around Philadelphia is similar to metropolitan Houston or Los Angeles; once you look past differences of climate and geography. The national standards used to build the interstate system produce similar highway configurations almost everywhere. Corporations expect the same characteristics in office buildings whether they are in Dallas, Dayton, or Denver. Much retailing is now dominated by national chains, and hotels belong to national franchise organizations. Airports serve the same airlines and rental car companies, and tend to be similar from place to place. National home-building and apartment developers construct the same houses and apartment types in many different markets. Public housing projects tend to look much the same from city to city, as they were built to the same administrative standards. The important differences among cities and towns come from their positions in the metropolitan region to which they belong. As David Rusk has documented, older cities like Philadelphia, Detroit, or St. Louis, which are unable to expand their boundaries, have more severe fiscal problems than cities like Houston or Phoenix that can grow by annexation. There is also a big difference between the Harlem district of Manhattan and Greenwich, Connecticut. But there are also great similarities among places that have comparable positions in their respective metropolitan regions. A distressed inner city neighborhood is going to have the same kinds of problems in Houston as those of a similar neighborhood in Baltimore or Philadelphia. And a country-club district outside of Boston won't look too different from one in Tulsa.

Sustainability is the most important issue relating to city and regional planning at the beginning of this new century. The basic sustainability question is about population. Will the number of people in the world stabilize at a level that will preserve the resources of the planet for future generations, without worldwide war, famine, or epidemics, and without changing the planetary ecosystem in ways that make it inhospitable to human life? Unfortunately, this issue is so sweeping in its implications and so far out of the control even of nations, much less individuals, that it is tempting to just tune it out.

The two opening chapters of this book offer a way to approach sustainability, admittedly incrementally, but nonetheless effectively, by pursuing policies that promote sustainability region by region. The metropolitan region is now the key unit of economic development in a global economy, explains Theodore Hershberg in the opening chapter. Strengthening regions is a necessary economic survival strategy, as well as the key to solving many other economic and social problems. Urban areas are already evolving into a new kind of regional city, as described by Gary Hack in Chapter 2, so the setting for these new policies has already changed in ways that some people do not yet recognize. Roger Raufer, in Chapter 5, describes how successes to date in air pollution control have brought about a shift from immediate public health issues to concerns about long-term environmental damage. Regulation to protect the environment requires looking at whole regions, as opposed to the local decisions and controls used to protect the public from pollution close to its sources. These broader-based concerns also require looking at the differences among regions and deciding what level of environmental protection makes economic sense. They also suggest using economic means for encouraging pollution control, as environmental issues can have significant effects on the larger economy. Anne Spirn in Chapter 11 analyzes parallel developments in controlling water pollution. With the relative success of measures to combat water pollution from sewage, the emphasis is changing to the control of pollutants in stormwater run-off, which Spirn suggests, can best be achieved by working with regional natural systems, rather than channeling run-off through pipes and pollution control plants.

Smart Growth and Livable Communities are both slogans that relate sustainability to regional and local issues. Urban sprawl is clearly a major sustainability issue. A new "green" house built on a mountainside with the latest in solar systems and natural pollution control—but needing extensions of road systems and services—is likely to be far more destructive of the environment than building a conventional house on a vacant lot in an established neighborhood. "Smart Growth" as a term has been promoted, particularly by the U.S. Environmental Protection Agency, to emphasize that regional and local planning policies to combat sprawl are not necessarily anti-growth. The Urban Land Institute, sponsored by real estate developers, and the National Association of Home Builders have both adopted Smart Growth to describe their policies. Growth has to happen, but there are good ways and bad ways for it to take place. A less widely accepted subtext is that rapid growth at the fringe of a slow-growing metropolitan region is not smart if it is drawing population and resources out of older areas. "Livable Communities," as promoted by the American Institute of Architects and other organizations, is a phrase that helps relate urban sprawl and other planning issues to the concerns of everyday life.

John Keene in Chapter 3 describes the extensive growth management policies already in place in more than one-fourth of the United States, plus other regional growth management measures, and relates them not only to sustainability for the environment but to social equity. This existing legislation has created a body of precedents and experience that can be drawn on by other states. In Chapter 4, I describe ways in which local governments can promote environmental preservation by rewriting zoning and subdivision codes to include environmental considerations. Local governments can also use their codes to create neighborhoods and compact, walkable commercial centers, instead of housing tracts and highway strip development. Smart growth, in these two chapters, is defined as restricting development at the metropolitan fringe, promoting reinvestment in older cities and towns, and making it easier to tie the new regional city together with rapid transit as well as highways, by making new development compact enough to be served by transit.

We have anticipated the usual response, which is that this kind of regional growth management is not possible until there are big improvements in both public safety and the school systems in older cities and towns, and that these older communities can't improve themselves until they get out from under their unequal share of social welfare spending. That is why we have included chapters on public safety, education, and welfare reform.

Thomas Seamon in Chapter 8 explains that the recent improvements in crime statistics are traceable at least in part to a more environmental and community-based approach to policing. Dealing immediately with broken windows, graffiti, and other seemingly minor ways in which a place can appear neglected and out of control seems to create an environment where crime is less likely to happen. Deploying the police in relation to locations of recent crimes, working with neighborhood organizations, and encouraging police officers to understand the communities where they are working, also help explain recent improvements in public safety. Rising crime statistics turn out not to be inevitable; if current trends continue, avoiding crime may no longer be a reason for moving away from cities, or deciding not to live and work there.

Education is a complex issue, made more complex as society has expanded education to make it more truly universal. Theodore Hershberg points out that, while public elementary and secondary schools may work better, on average, in suburban communities than in older cities, the performance of U.S. students in general does not compare well with students in other countries with advanced economies. Susan Fuhrman, in Chapter 7, urges policymakers to focus on improvements to instruction and investments in a broad range of educational needs, rather than looking to a quick fix from administrative measures like vouchers and charter schools, which won't increase the supply of qualified teachers or, by themselves, improve teaching methods.

Roberta Iversen in Chapter 9 disentangles the motivations behind the latest federal welfare reform and describes what administrative changes and additional policies will be needed to move large numbers of people off welfare permanently.

Given the fragmented structure of local government in most metropolitan regions, how would it be possible to implement smart growth policies? Stephen Putman explains in Chapter 6 that there is a de facto growth management and regional planning system at work in the United States today: the utilization forecast that is part of the planning process for every new highway. The priority, scope, and location of highway construction have a decisive effect on the future of each metropolitan area. Unfortunately, the utilization forecast is considered merely a technical procedure and is done by government officials or consultants who would be horrified to be told that they are doing planning. They are predicting the number of cars that will use the highway in the future but, despite statutory requirements that these forecasts take into account the new development that the highway will induce, Putman says that they almost never do so. And were they to predict induced development, what kind of development would they assume? Would it be smart growth or business as usual? Almost no one would know, as this kind of forecast is considered an administrative matter for the state highway department. So big decisions are made that affect the future of a whole region, without full understanding of their consequences, much less any public discussion of them. But the mechanism exists in every state department of transportation, and could become part of the basis for effective regional planning.

More specific livability issues are discussed in the concluding section of this book. Eugenie Birch, in Chapter 10, describes how old concerns about housing shortages and slum conditions have been alleviated, while leaving us with a serious problem of housing affordability. Most of the policies and programs to deal with this problem are in place but have not been funded at the necessary level. Housing affordability also relates to the points I make in Chapter 4 about changing local zoning codes to promote neighborhoods of diverse housing types, rather than large tracts of houses all at the same price.

Keeping older city centers competitive also turns on issues that can be described under the heading of livability. Paul Levy writes in Chapter 12 how business improvement districts like the one he directs for Center City Philadelphia can change the environment downtown, making it cleaner, safer, and more welcoming to workers and visitors. Anne Spirn also addresses livability issues, demonstrating how urban neighborhoods have deteriorated because all or part of them were built in locations that should never have been developed, because they were wetlands and watercourses. Restoring natural systems in these areas has a double benefit: providing a good way of dealing with stormwater run-off and creating parklands comparable to the natural environment people are seeking when they move to suburbs.

Of course these are just examples of the way this book seeks to relate the most recent academic research to current public policy concerns. We have tried to make the text as accessible as possible, without diluting its content. Each chapter follows a similar outline: first the issues are identified, then there is a background briefing, which is followed by specific policy suggestions. There are also suggestions for additional reading. We hope you will find it a useful resource for some important public policy questions.

The New Metropolitanism

Chapter 1

Regional Imperatives of Global Competition

Theodore Hershberg

The Global Economy, Regions, and Regional Cooperation

Americans are growing more aware of the metropolitan areas or regions in which they live. This new consciousness is developing in metros as diverse as San Francisco, Portland, Phoenix, Denver, Austin, New Orleans, Atlanta, Chicago, Philadelphia, Baltimore, and Buffalo. It is accompanied by an interest in regional cooperation because, in the absence of regional government, this strategy makes it possible for central cities and their surrounding communities to seize opportunities in a timely fashion and solve problems that cut across the political boundary lines that separate them.

This growing interest in regions and regional cooperation springs from many sources. There is recognition that the solutions for many serious problems facing cities are embedded in metropolitan contexts. The devolution from federal to state governments of both decision-making authority and funding has persuaded many people that cities and their surrounding suburban communities stand a much better chance of securing these funds and policy controls if they work together as a region than by competing with each other.

As cities and suburban communities realize that the de facto economic development strategies of the past three decades—federal spending on health care and defense—have stopped generating substantial numbers of new jobs, they have begun to collaborate on strategies to move their regions in new economic directions. Particularly in the Midwest and the Northeast, where suburban economic growth has been sluggish because the steady flow of jobs and people out of central cities over the past thirty years has finally slowed, business leaders have taken a new interest in regional economic development strategies.

But persuasive as these arguments may be, they pale in significance next to the importance of the global economy in explaining the sharply growing interest in regional thinking and regional action. When historians chronicle the last quarter of the twentieth century, they will be unanimous in concluding that its defining phenomenon was the emergence of the global economy. In 1960, imports and exports equaled 11 percent of the American economy. By 1990, they accounted for 25 percent and, by that decade's end, they exceeded 30 percent. America already exports 33 percent of its total agricultural output. Imports and exports account for 40 percent of *Fortune* 500 company profits and 20 percent of corporate profits overall. Forty percent of commercial loans are made by foreign lenders and 30 percent of automobiles sold here are made abroad. Between 1992 and 1997—that is, before the economic slowdown in Asia—one in every three new jobs in America was created in the export sector. Ten percent of the nation's $6 trillion in private pension funds are invested in Asian companies alone. Whether one embraces or laments these changes, the evidence makes clear that the global economy has arrived and is expanding rapidly.

Three major forces drive the global economy. The first is free trade. Although it is more accurate to say "managed trade"—ways of regulating and taxing the goods and services that flow across national borders—the long-term trend is unmistakably toward eliminating barriers and creating free markets worldwide.

The second force is global capital markets. Money is the lifeblood of business and vast flows of funds now characterize the global economy. Although the value of goods and services in the American economy totals roughly $8 trillion annually, every working day $2 trillion circulate electronically among banks around the world. Although it remains easier to acquire venture capital from domestic lenders, for the first time in modern history these funds are available on a global basis, meaning that money can now be found to finance good deals regardless of their location.

Third, we are in the midst of an extraordinary revolution in terms of communications and information technology, which has a lot to do with facilitating both global trade and global capital markets. To illustrate what is happening, Nicholas Negroponte, director of the media lab at the Massachusetts Institute of Technology, relates a story in his recent volume, *Being Digital.* A group of youngsters are asked whether they would choose a million dollars or a penny-a-day doubled for a month. Most immediately take the million dollars; the brighter students start counting on their fingers, but when they arrive at the middle of the month and their total is still in the low three digits, they too elect to take the million dollars. But if the month is February, the total is a bit more than $1 million; if the month is June, the total exceeds $5 million; and if the month is January—that is, a month with thirty-one days—the total is $10.37 million![1]

Why relate this story? The doubling occurs every day, Negreponte explains, but the payoff really comes at the close of the month. Up until now all the talk about the information superhighway has been a lot of hype, but as he points out, we have come at last to the "end of the month" where truly remarkable changes are under way.

The Internet is changing how people communicate and how commerce is conducted. Today 200 million people (112 million in America) are on the net, and this number is expected to reach 1 billion by 2003. Estimates for the value of "business to business" sales on the Internet in 2004 range from $2.4 trillion to $7.3 trillion, which helps to explain why Internet stocks are going through the roof. Our televisions, computers, and telephones, courtesy of new common digital standards, will soon be merged. Within six to ten years, technology will make it possible to link every person on the globe via low-orbit satellite and portable cell phones equipped to handle video and data as well as audio. The smartest people in corporations and institutions of all types around the globe are thinking about how to position their organizations to take full advantage of these remarkable changes.

The most important lesson the global economy teaches is that regions—not cities or counties—will be the units of economic competition. The view that regions are becoming the key units in the future is widely held.

According to Victor Petrella, chief of forecasting for the European Union, "Within 50 years, nation-states will no longer be the most relevant socioeconomic entities and the ultimate political configuration. The real decision-making power of the future will be transnational companies in alliance with city-regional governments." Kenichi Ohmae, a former partner at McKinsey & Co. and author of a dozen books on corporations and global trade, writes about it this way in *The End of the Nation State: The Rise of Regional Economies:* "The noise you hear rumbling in the distance is the sound of the later 20th century's primary engine of economic prosperity stirring to life. Companies will no longer organize their international activities on the basis of national borders. Region-states have become the primary units of economic activity through which participation in the global economy actually takes place."[2] Finally, Neal Peirce, the nationally syndicated columnist, and Curtis Johnson, his coauthor in "Peirce Reports" on seventeen American regions, explain it this way: "Only when the central city and its surrounding counties work together, will they be able to compete effectively. It won't be America vs. Japan or Germany, but Greater Philadelphia vs. metropolitan Stuttgart or metropolitan Lyon."[3]

Why are regions understood as the basic units of domestic and worldwide competition? The creation of goods and services depends upon key resources, labor force, transportation, infrastructure, and environment, each of which is *regional* in scope. In America, roughly half the commuting population in metropolitan areas crosses a county line each working day. Regions must cultivate a quality indigenous labor force, or by definition they become less competitive, because the higher wages employers have to pay to attract qualified labor from other regions increases their costs. All transportation networks—roads; highways, mass transit, and rail—are regional in scope. So, too, is the infrastructure, whether water mains or sewer lines or underground cable that carries digital signal. The environment can only be understood as a regional system. Neither polluted air nor contaminated water respect political boundary lines. They flow freely within watersheds and move with the prevailing winds.

Moreover, only regions have the scale and diversity to market goods and services on a global basis and to attract foreign investment. When growth or unemployment rates are reported for the nation, a single figure is provided. But these numbers are statistical averages of economic activity across hundreds of metropolitan statistical areas with significantly different rates. The national economy has always been understood as an aggregate expression of our many metropolitan economies, but in a global economy, where regions are the units of competition, it pays to focus more self-consciously on the health of specific regions.

Elected officials, economic development professionals, and corporate leaders share the desire to expand the tax base, increase the number of jobs, and grow the economy. But before creating strategies to achieve these ends, Russell Ackoff, professor emeritus at the Wharton School of the University of Pennsylvania, offers a critical distinction between "growth" and "development," terms that most people use interchangeably as synonyms. "Growth" is a concept concerned with size and expansion, he explains, but "development" is a concept concerned with competence and capacity building. This distinction is even more important in an era of dramatic change, such as today, when, as Peter Drucker argues, we are midway through two meta-transformations: from a domestic to a global economy and from an industrial to a post-industrial society. To maximize growth, we should think first about development—What new institutions must be put in place? How should we be repositioning ourselves? What new ways of looking at and thinking about the world are required to take advantage of this rapidly changing environment?

The region, as the unit of competition in the global economy, is itself a critical developmental concept, and regional thinking and regional action are key developmental approaches. This is why regional cooperation has become an indispensable strategy for the future.

The bad news for those promoting regional cooperation is there is no formula for swift success, which, if faithfully followed, will yield guaranteed results. First, the roots of our parochialism are deeply embedded in the soil of race, class, and politics, and, over a very long period of time, they have grown tough and very resistant to change. Even if a formula existed, it would be more an art than a science, more like a recipe for preparing béarnaise sauce than brewing tea. Second, it certainly would not be swift. And, third, there aren't many success stories—as in someone out there who's really done it and can say, "Okay, what's the next problem?"

The rate at which progress is being achieved depends largely on perspective. For activists working in "real time"—that is, day-in and day-out—progress can be painfully slow. But when examined over decades, excellent headway is being made. As few as fifteen years ago, with the notable exceptions of Minneapolis, Portland, and Toronto, "regional cooperation" existed largely as an oxymoron. The really good news today is that regional cooperation is on metropolitan radar screens all across the United States and that virtually every major region and many smaller ones are engaged in some sort of regional thinking and action. More often than not, these efforts are driven by the corporate community, with involvement from the civic and public sectors. But regardless of who leads, regions will do best when all three groups are at the table.

The global economy can be likened to a great train coming through every region in the world, and each region must decide on the kind of station needed for getting on or off the train. Regions that learn to act cohesively and can transcend parochial thinking and find ways to overcome the formidable barriers of race, class, and politics, will do much better than regions whose business, political, and civic leaders are unable to work together.

The global economy poses four major challenges to every region:

1. Develop your human resources because people will be the basis of comparative advantage in the future.
2. Lower the cost of your goods and services because the global economy is characterized by fierce competitiveness.
3. Use your scarce investment capital wisely, which, among other things, means reducing or eliminating the costly redundancies and waste created by suburban sprawl.
4. Stabilize the core city of each region because in no place is there evidence of regions doing well when their core city has deteriorated.

Develop Human Resources

The development of human resources is without reservation the most important challenge facing regions. Everything else can be gotten right—the best land use policies, outstanding arts, culture and related amenities, and a highly efficient transportation network—but if a region lacks a skilled labor force, its future is bleak.

The floor on which Americans have been standing for the last twenty years has been tilting, and people without real skills have been sliding toward reduced wage levels. The angle of tilt grows inexorably sharper each year as global trade and technology advance. If our children and grandchildren are to be secured to firm economic ground in the future, they must be provided with lifelines that are fashioned of far higher skill and education than was ever required in the past.

Although the American economy is doing exceedingly well in aggregate terms, not all American families are sharing in the rewards of this growth. According to the U.S. Census of Income, over the past twenty years, the bottom three-fifths of families have actually lost ground and the second-to-highest fifth has made modest gains. The top fifth, in contrast, have gained 25 percent and the top 5 percent have gained 44 percent.[4]

This distribution of income represents growing inequality, a significant departure from the pattern established in the decades following World War II. In December 1994, the Federal Reserve Bank of New York convened a panel of eighteen prominent economists and asked them to explain the sources of income inequality. Their consensus response was that 9 percent resulted from the erosion of the minimum wage; 10 percent from the decline of labor unions; and 10–20 percent from growing global competition—simply put, when faced with low-cost and decent-quality goods and services created abroad, American employers hold down the wages they pay to their workers (which in large part is why we can have 4 percent national unemployment and no inflation to speak of). But the economists attributed fully half of the explanation for growing income inequality to "new technologies that favor the better educated."

American schools always did a good job with the top fifth of their students. What happened to the remaining 80 percent did not matter because they went out into a robust manufacturing economy and received middle-class sustaining wages for relatively limited skills. Through the 1940s and 1950s and to 1964, the typical blue-collar worker earned enough for Mom to stay at home and raise the kids, and there was enough money left over for a second car.

The typical worker in 1973 earned higher real wages than the typical worker in 1997. But our standard of living did not fall because this decline in wages was softened and obscured by the entry of unprecedented numbers of women into the labor force, creating two-income families where the earnings of one had sufficed in the past. The "rubber band" has been stretching, with Americans working longer hours and holding more jobs than they have in a generation. But absent polygamy, there will be no third spouse to send into the labor force to bail out families in the next decade.

The report of the Commission on the Skills of the American Workforce, *America's Choice: High Skill or Low Wages!*, explains why the days of a robust manufacturing economy are never coming back. If companies all over the world can buy the same foolproof machinery to compensate for deficient worker skills, and billions of people around the world will use that machinery for $5 or $10 *a day*, let alone the $10 or $15 *per hour* plus benefits that American workers want, the moral of the story is clear. You cannot compete on the basis of wage, you can compete only on the basis of skill.[5]

American schools, for well over a century, did an extraordinary job of preparing their students for the industrial labor market. They took millions of immigrants and rural migrants and taught them to show up on time, develop a work ethic, respect authority, and repeat monotonous tasks. In brief, they socialized an entire population to the discipline of the factory system. In large measure because our "command and control" schools were so perfectly aligned with the needs of our manufacturing economy, America became an industrial superpower.

But workers in the post-industrial era require a very different set of skills. Driven by rapid technological change, the new global economy dictates that our schools graduate students who are flexible, adaptable, quick learners, critical thinkers, team players, and problem solvers. This will necessitate changes in our entire human capital development system, not simply our K–12 schools. A brief overview of this system, from K–12 through post-secondary training, higher education, and on-the-job is in order.

Most suburban residents compare their schools to those of the big cities they surround. Because on average they have lower dropout rates, better achievement scores, and higher college enrollment rates, suburbanites conclude that their schools are fine and that the problems reside in the cities. Unfortunately, there is no comfort in this suburban-to-urban school comparison. Worse, this comparison functions as a sedative, a soporific that has put Americans to sleep. It has left us complacent, thinking that the education problem lies elsewhere, in our cities with their large, poor, disproportionately nonwhite populations. The more accurate comparisons are those of American students with their future competitors growing up in the nations of western Europe and the Pacific Rim. Ample evidence from the National Academy of Science's *Third International Math and*

Science Study and the results from the internationally benchmarked, problem-solving exams (New Standards Reference Exams) developed by the national New Standards Project make clear that nowhere in America—not even in our best school districts—are the majority of students performing at world-class levels.[6]

The Federal Bureau of Labor Statistics describes the educational profile of new jobs created in 2000 as follows: 15 percent will need only high school diplomas; 30 percent will need college degrees; and the remainder will require some sort of post-secondary vocational training. Yet for every $1 of taxpayer money we spend on post-secondary training where most new jobs will be, we spend $55 subsidizing college students. The United States is unique in the world in not having an organized post-secondary training system for the non–college bound.

America has 3,600 colleges and universities: 2,200 four-year and the balance in two-year schools. While our elite universities are the best in the world, some estimates suggest that fewer than 600 of these institutions reject applicants on the basis of academic achievement, which is to say that as long as students can pay tuition they can attend and graduate from college. The result, according to a German executive quoted in the *America's Choice* report, is that "America has too many people in college and not enough qualified workers. America has outstanding universities, but it is missing its middle."[7] Estimates that one of every four students in a community college in this country already holds a baccalaureate degree suggest that many of these colleges add precious little value to the skill set of their graduates. They are enrolled in community colleges because when they entered the labor market to find a job, no one would hire them because they had no marketable skills. The "era of credentials" in higher education, when a degree rather than genuine skills was all that was required to find a job, is coming to an end.

The American Society for Training and Development reports that American companies spent about $30 billion in 1992 on formal training. But $27 billion was accounted for by 15,000 large corporations, roughly 5 percent of all U.S. employers, and two-thirds of this was spent not on ordinary workers on the shop floor who must assume new responsibilities after down-sizing middle managers, but to senior people being tracked for positions at the very top of these organizations.

Changes are required throughout our human capital development system, but reforming K–12 education is key. At the National Education Summit (March 1996), forty-one of the nation's governors and forty-nine chief executive officers of the nation's largest corporations concluded that the top priority for America's schools was the adoption of rigorous academic standards and internationally benchmarked assessments.

Forty-nine states are now raising the bar of academic achievement and adopting high-stakes tests. But rigorous standards and tougher tests *alone* will neither create the thinking, problem-solving workforce required by the new economy nor close the gap between American students and those growing up in western European and Pacific Rim nations.

The critical ingredient is pedagogy—how we teach students—and the pedagogy of standards reform is revolutionary. In graduate school, student teachers read Dewey and Piaget and other progressive educators. But when they get to America's K–12 schools, the dominant theory of learning they find is rooted in memorization. Dating from the 1920s, this approach is characterized by the phrase "pathways to knowledge." Students learn through drill—dig the mental trench and then run the stuff repeatedly through it until it's learned.

But because the new economy changes with striking rapidity, students can no longer memorize a set of facts and be done with it. Workers are now required who can think and learn on their own. Lauren Resnick, a leading scholar of learning research, offers a contrasting approach characterized by the phrase "habits of mind."[8]

In this pedagogy students are purposefully trained to ask questions, make predictions, and use evidence to draw conclusions. It is a process through which, at the earliest ages, reasoning is taught and habits of mind are developed that enable students to become far more capable learners and thinkers. It is not memorization *versus* thinking (all subjects require mastery of facts), but memorization *and* thinking.

This pedagogy will make it possible for all children to achieve at high levels, but success depends on two indispensable interventions. First, the nation's entire teacher corps must be retrained to use the new problem-solving pedagogy in their classrooms. But instead of professional development characterized by random college courses or expert lectures to teacher-filled auditoriums, we need small groups of teachers, working collaboratively and guided by the new principles of learning, to improve instruction and student performance. This massive retraining of the nation's teacher corps will take many years and be very costly. But since there is little evidence that more money alone leads to educational improvements, let's tie this investment to a system of accountability that measures outputs—what students learn—rather than inputs.

Second, we must hold educators accountable for the performance of their students. As long as teachers' contracts buy essentially only the number of days per year they appear in a classroom, human nature suggests that too few teachers will embrace retraining. But if performance contracts and incentive pay are adopted widely—Denver and Seattle offer examples—enough teachers will make the long-term commitment required to master the new pedagogy.

Opinion polls show strong public support for performance contracts for teachers and administrators. Union leadership is split between those who believe their only focus should be on salary and benefits, the "bread and butter" issues of industrial unions, and those who see future teachers as "united mind workers" who can lead the Information Age and accept responsibility for value-added performance.

In most communities, the local real estate tax cannot support the added cost of incentives and professional development. The teachers' unions should be offered a quid pro quo: in return for their acceptance of performance contracts that are fair to educators and credible to the public, school funding will be shifted to the state's personal income tax. This is going to happen anyway because when the politically powerful "baby-boomers" retire on fixed incomes; they won't tolerate real estate taxes.[9]

In the twenty-first century, human capital will be *the* source of comparative advantage. These critical reforms in teaching, accountability, and funding will ensure that our children and grandchildren will be able to compete effectively in a world far, far different from the one in which we grew up.

Lower the Costs of Goods and Services

The second challenge the global economy poses to regions is the need to lower the costs of their goods and services. The good news about the global economy is that the market is so vast: 6 billion potential consumers. The bad news is that Americans are competing for profit and market share with firms around the world.

People who have worked in government acknowledge widespread inefficiencies embedded in the configuration of local, state, county, and federal governments: duplicated personnel, facilities, and service, and limited management incentives. These inefficiencies result in higher taxes and increased business costs.

The question is why business has not complained about this and insisted that it change. The answer lies in the workings of a domestic economy—business passes the costs of these inefficiencies on to customers in the form of higher prices, thereby leaving the profit margins unaffected. And business can do this without competitive consequences because all producers in a domestic economy do the same thing. It is inefficient, to be sure, but in the past it didn't matter.

Now it does. A global economy changes everything. When the competition grows increasingly international and, for whatever reasons, foreign goods and services of decent quality and low cost enter the domestic marketplace, American employers must change past practices to remain competitive. In *World Class: Thriving Locally in the Global Economy,* Harvard Business School professor Rosabeth Moss Kantor illustrates the nature of global competition through the experience of a small American envelope manufacturer.[10] The company learns that the contract it has long held with a large local corporation has just been won by a Taiwanese competitor who provided a quality product at a lower price. After streamlining its internal operations, the local company reviews further options to stay competitive: it can reduce its profits; it can lower the wages of its workers; or it can look outside the firm to find ways to lower its costs.

The same fiscal discipline triggered by the global economy that corporate America has been going through for the past decade, and which is now eviscerating the health care industry, will affect every institution in the nation, and there is no reason to believe government will be spared. Moreover, as voters, workers, and their families understand the choice they face in order to maintain the competitiveness of American goods and services in a global economy—either to lower their wages or to find other ways of reducing costs—they will not surprisingly choose the latter. Government practices considered sacrosanct today will change far more rapidly than most people now appreciate because politicians will quickly grasp that Americans are more committed to their wallets than to abstract notions of traditional local governance.

The response should not be ideological, in which the region automatically becomes the appropriate unit for the delivery of services. Rather, regions should be asking what size "service shed" is appropriate for individual services and, for that matter, whether government should produce the service or contract it out to the private sector. Regions should be using cost-benefit analysis to blow away the political smoke that obscures more rational choices. The issue is not structural, requiring the consolidation of governments into larger units, but functional, offering services at the most efficient geographic scale. Efforts to tackle this politically sensitive subject are under way in several regions, including promising starts catalyzed by the State University of New York in Buffalo and the Rockefeller Institute of Government at the State University of New York in Albany.[11]

Use Scarce Investment Capital Wisely

The third challenge posed to regions by the global economy is to use their scarce investment capital wisely. Exurban development—more popularly known as "suburban sprawl"—represents wasteful and redundant spending. When crime, drugs, homelessness, and other social problems spill over into adjacent suburban communities, the response of those who can afford it has been to move even farther away to more pristine areas at the peripheries of our regions. This process is embedded in the concentric rings of growth that emanate from our central cities.

Very troubling signs in the older, inner-ring suburbs suggest that the pace of out-migration and other indicators of deterioration—job loss, housing depreciation, drugs, crime, and related social problems—is accelerating faster than in the central cities they surround. In *Metropolitics,* Myron Orfield explains why. These small communities lack the basic resources big cities rely on to slow down and mediate the process of decline. These inner-ring communities do not have large central business districts generating substantial tax revenues to underwrite essential services in the neighborhoods; they do not have large police forces to maintain safety and a sense of social order as the crime rate climbs; and they do not have the sizeable public and not-for-profit social service agencies to address the needs of the poor and disadvantaged.[12]

When people leave the inner-ring suburbs, they are not going to the second or even the third ring out, but to the exurbs. Between 1970 and 1995, southeastern Pennsylvania—Philadelphia and the four suburban counties that comprise the Pennsylvania side of the metro region—lost 140,000 people and one-quarter of its highly productive farmland. The city of Lancaster, Pennsylvania, houses its 60,000 residents in 7 square miles. But the County of Lancaster, which added 60,000 residents between 1980 and 1990, required 77 square miles to house the newcomers. New Jersey has more land in cultivation as lawn than in agriculture.

The conversion of farmland to residential communities is a very costly process. An entire infrastructure must be built: roads and bridges, water lines and sewer mains, shopping centers and office complexes, homes and schools, and libraries and hospitals. When this happens, our scarce investment dollars are spent redundantly because we are essentially duplicating an infrastructure that already exists in older suburbs and central cities.

This redundant spending imposes heavy opportunity costs because these dollars are not available for more vital investments to increase productivity in human capital or plant and equipment. While Americans are building shopping centers, the Japanese are investing in research and development. In November 1998, in what took most antisprawl advocates by surprise, two-thirds of roughly 200 ballot initiatives to limit sprawl were approved by voters across the nation. After extensive polling and focus groups, Vice President Gore concluded that curbing sprawl had emerged as a viable national issue on which to campaign for the presidency.

David Rusk's newest book, *Inside-Game, Outside-Game: Winning Strategies for Saving Urban America,* argues that opponents of sprawl and inner-city activists have much in common because they are partners in a regional system. By joining forces politically, they can support both "brownfield" legislation to redevelop the cities and open space initiatives to preserve suburban land.[13] To improve the nation's competitive position in the global economy, America's regions would be far wiser to undertake more cost-effective development by adopting land use and growth management controls, increasing residential and job densities in existing suburbs and cities, and investing the savings in research and development, plant and equipment, and human capital.

America should not behave in the 2000s as it did in the 1960s. The current practice of redundant spending is akin to eating our seed corn. The nation can ill afford public policy that leads to throwaway cities, throwaway suburbs, and throwaway people.

Stabilize the Region's Core City

The fourth challenge of the global economy to regions is to stabilize their core cities. Despite the recent comeback of America's downtowns, most cities are on greased skids, and what distinguishes one from the other is the angle of descent. The next recession will make painfully clear just how fragile the recent gains have been. How can thoughtful people believe America will emerge a stronger nation when we have lost most of our big and medium-size cities and have not simply the same social problems, but ones much worse for having festered unattended?

Why is it that suburbanites seem content to stand by, watching their central city slide down the skids? Here are two propositions to ponder. First, perhaps they don't appreciate the degree of economic self-interest at stake in the decline of their central city. The argument is not that the suburbs will be destroyed by atomic blast if the city declines, but rather that there will be substantial fall out. For example, the growth of Detroit's suburbs has been considerably slower in terms of population, jobs, and personal income than that of suburbs that surround healthier central cities in the Midwest and the Northeast.

Or consider who loses when the value of urban real estate declines. According to researchers at the Wharton School's Real Estate Center, the value of all real estate in ten of America's biggest cities is about $1.6 trillion. Suppose we accelerate depreciation and write off 10 percent—$160 billion—of this total. It turns out that the losers are not primarily the folks who live in cities, but suburbanites. Why? Because they are the dominant shareholders in the banks, insurance companies, and pension funds that own the big downtown office complexes, which account for the lion's share of the value of urban real estate.

Arguments like these—demonstrating suburban economic self-interest—are like arrows in a quiver. While it is useful to have more to shoot at skeptical targets, more arguments documenting economic self-interest may not be what is needed to convince suburbanites to get involved. Evidence from metropolitan Philadelphia suggests another approach. An annual telephone opinion survey undertaken from 1996 to 1999 reveals that most suburbanites are aware of the interdependencies with their central city; they already believe their future economic and social conditions will be seriously affected by Philadelphia's decline. Suburbanites expressed similar views in over thirty focus groups conducted by graduate students at the University of Pennsylvania in the last decade.

Suburbanites are passively watching Philadelphia slide down the greased skids not because they fail to recognize their moral obligation, nor because they're unaware of the considerable economic self-interest they have in the city's well-being. They're not getting involved, rather, because they believe decades of federal interventions failed, proving that the city's problems are intractable and that city politicians are too prone to mismanagement and corruption to sustain long-term reform. They stand by and watch because they don't know what else to do. They see it as some sort of a Greek tragedy.

The Wharton Real Estate Center research concluded that the nation's cities suffer from three structural problems. First, their tax base has shrunk over the past forty years with the exodus of jobs and people and the significant reduction in federal funds. Second, as a result, a mismatch has emerged: Funds available to cities from all sources are insufficient to cover the costs of the social problems of the poverty populations that live within their borders. Although the federal government reimburses localities for expenses related to alleviating poverty using a per-capita allocation, the Wharton research documents that the greater the concentration of poverty, the more expensive it becomes to deliver services such as fire, health, police, and education. For every point that the local poverty rate exceeds the national poverty rate, it costs a local taxpayer in Philadelphia $23—a total of $241 million—or a burden to local taxpayers of 10 percent of the annual city budget. In short, cities cannot solve their problems on their own. As outgoing mayor Ed Rendell puts it, "When I became mayor, I inherited a patient suffering from gunshot wounds and cancer. I have successfully addressed the gunshot wounds, but my patient is going to die of cancer eventually because I don't have the resources available here to treat it. No matter how squeaky-clean a good-government machine mayors may make their cities, they cannot win this battle without more intergovernmental aid."

The third factor cities suffer from, according to the Wharton researchers, is misuse of the funds they do have, and it helps to explain why suburbanites are reluctant to help. The historical record suggests that although cities engage in reform during moments of fiscal crisis and political scandal, they have proven unable to sustain these reforms over time. When the energy that held the reform coalition together dissipates, the politicians return to their usual practices.

If suburbanites believe cities won't reform themselves and cannot reform themselves without new funds from outside, then the time has come to engage them in a discussion of rational incentives to induce permanent changes achieved through outside intervention. This could take the form of a dialogue to identify precisely what the city should do to be worthy of suburban support in the state capitol. Simply put: state money to leverage urban reform. The following examples are based on focus groups conducted in Philadelphia's suburbs, but they should be applicable in many regions.

Suburbanites showed strong support for three actions which, if taken by city's political leaders, could result in a new quid pro quo: in exchange for real urban reform, the state would make additional funds available to help the city with the burden imposed by its high poverty populations.

Education Reform

If the Philadelphia Federation of Teachers accepts a performance-based contract that measures outcomes—value added over the course of the school year—and agreed upon academic progress is made, then substantial new funds would be given to the schools. Everyone in the region and the state would gain if the Philadelphia schools graduate students with the skills to secure jobs in the new economy.

City Services

Suburbanites believe there's too much waste. If Philadelphia requires every service to be competitively bid, including the hauling of trash so private sector firms could do the work, the city would receive additional funds. The bid specifications could insist that the work be done by union labor—because savings shouldn't come at the expense of working people, and in the case of trash the Teamsters could do the hauling—but carried out under private-sector management. If city workers win the bid, that's fine too, just as long as the savings are made.

Salaries and Benefits

The third action addresses the complaint voiced by many suburbanites that the salary and benefit packages negotiated by the city's unions are too high when measured against comparable work performed in the private sector elsewhere in the region. Suburbanites see mayoral and city council candidates too beholden for electoral support to the city's unions—teachers, police, fire, and blue- and white-collar government employees—to be able to exercise real control over wage and benefit levels. So if the city establishes a blue-ribbon panel of business leaders to arrive at pay benchmarked to comparable work in the private sector across the metropolitan area, Philadelphia would receive new funds.

When suburbanites recognize their economic self-interest in the well-being of their core city, a "rational incentive approach" can move them from passive observers of a "Greek tragedy" to active players in catalyzing and sustaining urban reform. Although such an approach may appear radical, there is much precedent for it—strings are always attached to federal monies, so why not negotiate some to attach to state money won with suburban support?

Why These Regional Issues Are So Urgent

The barriers to regional cooperation—race, class, and politics—are indeed formidable and it is along these lines that our society, our cities, and our suburbs are divided. Cities are home disproportionately to nonwhite Americans; indeed, most cities have nonwhite majorities. Cities house the nation's poor; their median incomes are two-thirds of those in the suburbs. Voters in cities are registered disproportionately—two, and even three and four to one—as Democrats, and in the suburbs, similar ratios favor Republicans. Given these striking differences, regional cooperation becomes a metaphor for the many issues of economic and social reform facing the nation.

Two demographic facts loom large over America's future. Between 1995 and 2020, the nation's population will grow by 60 million people, 47 million of whom will be African Americans, Latinos, and Asians. As a result, by 2020, 45 percent of all children under 18 will be nonwhite. They are growing up in the nation's worst environments and attending our worst schools. Most white Americans, living in the most racially and economically segregated society in our history, behave as if they were oblivious to these trends.

Regional cooperation may be the most difficult approach, but it is the right approach to dealing with America's problems. There are times when I tremble for the future of the nation because I recall the words of George

Kennan: "History will not excuse the inadequacy of response because of the enormity of the challenge."

NOTES

1. Nicholas Negroponte, *Being Digital* (New York: Knopf, 1995).

2. Kenichi Ohmae, *The End of the Nation State: The Rise of Regional Economies* (New York: Free Press, 1995).

3. Neal R. Peirce, with Curtis W. Johnson and John Stuart Hall, *Citistates: How Urban America Can Prosper in a Competitive World* (Washington, D.C.: Seven Locks Press, 1993).

4. Jason DeParle, "Class Is No Longer a Four-Letter Word," *New York Times Magazine,* March 17, 1996.

5. Commission on the Skills of the American Workforce, *America's Choice: High Skills or Low Wages* (Rochester, N.Y.: National Center on Education and the Economy, 1990).

6. William H. Schmidt, Curtis C. McKnight, and Senta A. Raizen, *A Splintered Vision: An Investigation of U.S. Science and Mathematics Education* (Boston: Kluwer Academic Publishers, 1997).

7. Commission on the Skills of the American Workforce, 1990.

8. Lauren Resnick and M. G. Hall, "Learning Organizations for Sustainable Education Reform," *Daedalus* (November 1998).

9. Ted Hershberg, "Long-Term Skills for Quick-Turn Tech," *Visions: Building Digital Government in the 21st Century,* supp. to *Government Technology* magazine (May 2000).

10. Rosabeth Moss Kantor, *World Class: Thriving Locally in the Global Economy* (New York: Simon and Schuster, 1995).

11. "Assessing Regionalism in Erie County," from *Governance in Erie County: A Foundation for Understanding and Action,* The Governance Project, State University of New York at Buffalo (January 1996); "Growing Together Within the Capital Region," from *The Draft Report of the State Commission on the Capital Region* (February 1996).

12. Myron Orfield, *Metropolitics: A Regional Agenda for Community Stability* (Washington, D.C.: Brookings Institution Press, 1997).

13. David Rusk, *Inside Game, Outside Game: Winning Strategies for Saving Urban America* (Washington, D.C.: Brookings Institution Press, 1999).

C h a p t e r   2

Planning Metropolitan Regions

Gary Hack

When we think about the future of metropolitan areas, it is not very useful to envision them as cities surrounded by a ring of suburbs. The terms "city" and "suburb" are themselves too limited to describe urban patterns as we move into the next century. We have to begin thinking about cities as metropolitan regions, or city regions, as a matrix of development that extends over wide areas and includes many centers. Some centers may have a longer history than others, but the original central city will not necessarily have a dominant position in the new metropolitan region. The Phoenix metropolitan region is one prototype of an area where the historic center is not the most important location, even for commerce. In Los Angeles, downtown is just one of many centers; in Atlanta, the areas known as Midtown, Buckhead, and Perimeter Center rival the importance of downtown, and political boundaries are not obvious on the ground.

Giving a Name to New Regional Realities

Calling the settled area that spans Pennsylvania, Delaware, and New Jersey "Philadelphia" is no longer accurate, as the region includes other cities, like Camden and Wilmington, and counties in the three states. The inelegant term "PenJerDel" may not have caught on, but more and more people are using the term Delaware Valley for the region. Most advertising for the Dallas–Fort Worth area refers to it as the Metroplex, although this term is also used in various places around the country for sports stadiums and convention centers. Miami is part of Metro-Dade, and around San Francisco it is the Bay Area. These new names reflect the new realities.

What's Wrong with Current Development?

Over the past several decades, much has been written that is critical of the sprawling form of the new metropolis. The policy debate has often assumed that there is a zero-sum game in which central areas and outlying areas compete for a limited pool of resources and do battle over each new locational decision. Urban sprawl has become defined as evil, and is a hot button for many politicians, appealing to an unlikely coalition of center city advocates, farmland preservationists, and designers interested in traditional forms of urban development.

As the new metropolitan region is here to stay, we need to be clear about what is wrong with the emerging development patterns. They are, of course, not new: For a century and a half, since the introduction of railroads, which allowed easy commuting from garden suburbs, there has been worry over the ever expanding perimeter of cities. Today, as older areas are deserted for new development on the urban fringe, it may be an inefficient use of public resources to let excess infrastructure lie fallow at the centers of cities while constructing new utilities as part of developments at the perimeter. When lengthening travel times and congestion in a metropolitan area make it uncompetitive and unattractive to people, the sprawling form of the city certainly becomes a problem. Individuals and businesses locate still further out to avoid congestion until, as Charles Tiebout so aptly observed, congestion equalizes itself. Dispersal can also be a problem if the infrastructure of sewers, water supply, roads, and transit can't support development at the new regional scale—although, if densities are low enough, collective water and sewer systems may not be a necessity.

There is often a mismatch between the location of jobs in the dispersed metropolis and those in need of employment. There may be a second disparity between the ability of public jurisdictions to raise resources through the forms of taxation they have available and the demands for services and social assistance placed upon them. The latter is a problem of governmental organization, not particularly an issue of urban form. And the supposition that every part of a region must be closely tied to the historic center is not necessarily the only, or even the most desirable, way for regions to develop.

Because of the way that most metropolitan regions have evolved, road and transit systems are often incongruous with the new geography. There are usually good radial expressways but poor circumferential highways, although only a small fraction of trips may be between center and periphery. There are few mass transit systems running between suburbs or between older communities at the fringe. Over the next generation, planning of such roads and rail lines, as well as new mass transit systems that connect radial routes, will become very important. Many of the proposals in the recent regional plan for New York advocate this, and in the Delaware Valley metropolitan area a mass transit system is being planned linking Camden and Trenton, New Jersey, parts of the region that are outside the traditional center. We will see a lot more of these kinds of projects.

The Evolution of "Sprawl" into New Patterns

People talk about suburban sprawl as if metropolitan areas were all developing at a uniform, low density. In fact, the evolving metropolitan region has a distinct underlying structure. Employment and shopping clusters have grown up in portions of metropolitan areas that have good highway access. Joel Garreau calls them Edge Cities, although they are not usually on the outer edge of the metropolitan region. Often these clusters include offices, services, shopping, hotels, entertainment areas—all the functions of an old city center, except that you can't get from one building to another without getting into your car. A major order of business for the next generation will be turning these clusters into functioning urban centers.

The next development opportunities in these clusters will involve the huge areas that have been set aside for parking. Decanting the parking into garages will open up land for additional businesses, housing, and facilities, and will create an opportunity for making the connections that are not there today. The difficulty is that all the highways leading to the cluster are likely to be congested already. Local governments resist approving more density unless there are new transportation systems, and a number of developers have begun to create transportation management organizations in suburban clusters. But if the new development is residential and thus has a different traffic pattern, or if the new development is for entertainment uses that encourage office workers to stay beyond the peak hour, it may not result in more congestion, and might well take advantage of otherwise vacant parking. Another way to reduce traffic congestion is by cutting the number of internal trips within the cluster. This can be accomplished by creating mixed-use areas that allow people to go to lunch and run other errands on foot. As a result, daytime traffic congestion should diminish.

The conundrum of emerging commercial clusters is that they cannot become true urban centers without mass transit and much higher densities, yet they cannot get government approval for such changes because of worries about congestion and spillover effects in adjacent areas. A breakthrough strategy may involve a combination of aggressive transportation management measures, locating new public facilities such as schools and cultural facilities in clusters, and creating new public–private arrangements, such as public parking authorities that can build garages that free up parking lots for added density.

Anne Vernez Moudon, has documented another type of suburban cluster that can be found in most metropolitan areas. These emerge in an unplanned way as communities map zones for garden apartments and town houses near arterial streets that have been zoned for strip shopping centers and franchise stores. Occasionally there are small office buildings along these commercial strips. There are often no connections among these assorted developments and frequently no sidewalks along the streets, but people create pathways across parking lots or undeveloped areas or lawns wherever they can. These clusters have all the ingredients of a traditional urban neighborhood, except again, that it is difficult to go from one building to another without using a car. Replanning these suburban residential clusters should be another priority for the next generation, and in high growth areas, there is an opportunity to plan such areas as more urban places before they are developed. These clusters will become the key points of access for suburban transit systems.

Over the next generation, the traditional city center will no longer be the only venue for cultural and entertainment events. Increasingly, these will be dispersed to other parts of the metropolitan region, near where many of their patrons live. Performing arts centers have recently been created in a number of newer urban areas such as El Cerrito, California, and West Palm

Beach, Florida, as well as on university campuses in smaller communities and outlying areas. Theaters, concert halls, and other civic spaces can become some of the glue that holds lively and interesting new centers together.

The Future of Traditional Downtowns

As outlying centers acquire the advantages traditionally enjoyed by center cities, what can one say about the future of traditional downtowns? They will become even more specialized subcenters, certainly not the only centers or even the most dominant ones, but important nonetheless. Their comparative advantage will be found in the areas of tourism, conventions, communications, entertainment, health care services, higher education, governmental services, private businesses closely linked to governments (e.g., lawyers dealing with the courts), logistics-sensitive industries that value centrality, and specialized retailing. Private headquarters functions and financial services will continue to be a component, but in only a few cities will they dominate downtown. Central areas will also remain attractive to those who wish to live and work in close proximity and to groups who value convenience over space.

New Neighborhood Diversity

Only 25 percent of the housing market today is made up of households with two parents and school-age children. Three quarters of households are in some other category: single parents, single people without children, married couples whose children have left home, married couples who do not expect to have children, unrelated individuals living together, and so on. While inner city neighborhoods have always seemed quite diverse, the profile of people living in outlying communities has also become quite different from the typical image of 1950s suburbia.

Although all the houses in a neighborhood may look similar, a close look at mature suburbs will reveal considerable diversity. A single parent or a retiree on a fixed income may be house-rich but strapped for disposable income, while next door a young couple may have a relatively high income but have much of it committed to a mortgage. Upwardly mobile people may stay in their modest neighborhood to maintain friendships and schools. Many outlying residential areas are becoming much more racially mixed as more ethnic groups become capable of affording new housing.

It is also a mistake to stereotype new metropolitan development. Specialized districts are emerging in outlying parts of the metropolitan region. As examples, there are close knit but dispersed artist communities on the urban fringe (such as Bucks County in Pennsylvania); semi-rural communities centered on weekend farming or ranching or keeping horses on the edges of many cities; villages for people who work on the Internet and commute to a more urban location or an outlying office park once or twice a week; golf and recreation communities that may have been designed for retirees but today are a lifestyle option.

New Regional Diversity

We are also witnessing lifestyle-based specialization of metropolitan areas. Orlando, for example, is largely a tourism- and entertainment-based community. But it has also attracted a large number of retirees who perhaps locate there in the hope that their grandchildren will visit them. The area around Rochester, Minnesota, also pulls in a large number of retirees who want to be near the medical care offered by the Mayo Clinic. University communities are attractive to those who are footloose because of the range of cultural opportunities they offer, and there has been a growth in retirees around many former military base communities.

There are high-tech communities built around research and education that define new metropolitan forms. The Research Triangle in North Carolina is a classic case of a location planned to take advantage of the three major universities located in three nearby communities, and by spanning the area between them a new form of settlement has emerged. Another obvious example is Silicon Valley in California, which owes its original impetus to Stanford University, but now sprawls across two counties. Then there are locations for special kinds of manufacturing, such as the Route 202 corridor west of Philadelphia from Wilmington, Delaware, to New Brunswick, New Jersey, where almost all the major pharmaceutical companies in the United States are located. There are regional manufacturing centers as well, such as Smyrna, Tennessee, in the Nashville metropolitan region, where a whole series of automotive parts manufactures have located around the Nissan plant because of the just-in-time manufacturing practices.

Jean Gottmann argued, in his 1961 book *Megalopolis,* that the northeastern United States from Boston to Washington was becoming a continuous, multi-centered urban corridor. But he also noted that this trend had included a great deal of functional differentiation in the corridor. Any survey today would confirm Gottmann's findings and add that the functional distinctions he observed have intensified. Princeton, New Jersey, can provide a place for executives to live in a small town, rubbing shoulders with academics and commuting to New York or Philadelphia, or more likely to an office park along the roads that connect the two cities. Loudoun County in Virginia west of Washington, D.C., is becoming a center for high-tech businesses, supported by the fact that the Washington metropolitan area attracts highly educated people and provides a cultural setting where they wish to locate. Gottmann's argument is that each settlement functions as it does because of its geographic relationship to other urban areas in the northeast corridor. You couldn't move one somewhere else and expect it to function in the same way.

The daily and weekly geographic range of people in these linked settlements also appears to be expanding. Today many people live in more than one part of the region. East Hampton, Long Island, used to be a summer resort but many of its residents currently spend three days of each week there and four days in New York year round. As the need to be near a fixed base of employment declines, people can make different lifestyle choices, and areas previously too distant from business centers are witnessing a great deal of growth—Portland, Maine; Northampton, Massachusetts; Bucks County, Pennsylvania; Charlottesville, Virginia, among many others.

People can commute outbound as well as inbound, and increased numbers of people who seek urbanity are choosing to locate in central cities even though their jobs may be elsewhere. The parts of the older cities that are most successful today in attracting residents are the highest density, mixed-use districts and the low-density garden neighborhoods. Notably passed by are many medium-density neighborhoods 2 or 3 miles from the center that have few of the virtues of urban life and none of the advantages of green countryside. There is a growing interest in living in city centers that have cultural activities, shopping, restaurants, and entertainment within pedestrian range, and generous if often rundown housing. Child-free households, including many active elderly, seek out such areas. For the 25 percent of households with school age children, the single most important deterrent to moving to central areas has been the poor quality of schools. Charter schools may begin to address this issue.

Outside city centers, new housing being constructed is almost always at much lower densities than in previous years. In the Hough neighborhood in Cleveland, an area that burned during the riots of the 1960s, the city is making land available at low prices and providing tax abatements to people who wish to build new homes. Dozens of housing units, including many mansions, are under construction, and the neighborhood is becoming a near downtown garden neighborhood. It has many locational advantages; it is next door to major hospitals and cultural institutions and close to downtown employment. Clearly the tax advantages are an important incentive, but the transformation of a tough area like Hough would not have happened without the desire of many to live close to urban amenities. And Hough is not alone; in cities across the country centrally located garden neighborhoods are growing in popularity (e.g., Brookline in Massachusetts, Chestnut Hill in Philadelphia, Highland Park in Dallas, Oak Park in Chicago, Roland Park in Baltimore, Georgetown in Washington, River Oaks in Houston, among others). Densities are increasing in many of these areas, and they are becoming more diverse ethnically and economically than when originally settled. They provide an important model for the revival of the rim of declining areas that surround many historic centers.

In the United States, there is a long history of clustering of economic activities in traditional urban centers—steel in Pittsburgh, autos in Detroit, finance in New York, and so on. But it is important to note that the new economic clusters are almost entirely at the fringes of metropolitan areas, not at their centers. And there is significant dispute over the issue of whether a healthy center is essential to continued prosperity of suburban clusters, or the reverse, whether suburban growth and development guarantee revitalization of historic centers. The patterns of interdependence appear to be subtle.

Some people might move to an outlying area because it offers the richness of opportunities once found only in traditional city centers, others may be attracted to living on farms, and still others may be drawn by educational opportunities in the region. Planning policies for metropolitan areas have to recognize both the diversity of regions and the diversity within particular regions. There is no single prescription that fits each case; policies must emerge from each area's comparative advantages.

Regional Trends in Other Countries

In looking at what future metropolitan policies should be, it is useful to compare the initiatives being taken in other countries. Roger Simmonds and I have been leading a study of twelve diversified metropolitan areas around the world, distributed equally across the Americas, Europe, and Asia. Between 1960 and 1990, in all of the cities studied there was rapid urbanization accompanied by rapid motorization. Metropolitan regions spread, often beyond the control of local governments of the central cities. In all but two of the cases studied, the settlements became much less dense—with population densities in European urban areas declining by 50 percent or more. The two exceptions are Taipei and Tokyo. Taipei, which is rimmed by mountains, grew dramatically in density but not in area because of its topographic constraints. Tokyo became considerably more dense, in large part because of a deliberate policy of limiting the conversion of farmland to urban uses, and because high quality mass transportation was provided for the entire region. In Tokyo's central area alone, seven new subway lines are currently under construction.

What are cities around the world trying to do today to structure this growth? The prevailing idea of planners remains Ebenezer Howard's century-old notion of creating new towns, aimed at intercepting development destined for what is regarded as oversized urban centers. Howard's solution advocated decentralization, not to suburban areas, but to planned communities 50 or 100 kilometers away from the old urban cores, or to intermediate sized cities even more distant. Greenbelts or urban limit lines are used to enforce the perimeter of urbanization. The London and Paris regions are textbook examples of this approach, and cities like Singapore and Hong Kong have pursued similar strategies.

New towns require huge capital resources and consistent political will, exercised over fifteen- to twenty-year periods, which few countries, much less cities, can muster. In the rapidly developing world, there are many more examples of failed than successful attempts to pursue such strategies—including the Jakarta and Bangkok regions, where political instability and corruption in land markets and infrastructure decisions confounded plans for decentralization.

New Regional Strategies in Other Countries

In the United States, new privately developed communities have had mixed success, in large part because they were not tied to a deliberate strategy of restraining growth elsewhere in the region. With the exception of Portland, Oregon, metropolitan regions in the United States have generally lacked the governmental resources and policies essential to implement effective growth strategies. Piecemeal efforts in various areas have led to urban utility limit lines, farmland preservation measures, transfers of development rights to help intensify development, inclusionary housing programs, commercial tax revenue sharing schemes, regional growth compacts, and various other restraints on the timing and location of development. Any region capable of marshaling all of these measures in an organized way could have considerable impact on the form of metropolitan development. But as piecemeal efforts, they have fallen far short of the detailed intervention needed to change land markets and developer behavior.

By contrast, a number of European and Canadian cities have restructured their forms of government to grant powers to regional entities to control infrastructure and the form and timing of development. As an example, the regional government of Madrid—whose powers were recently enlarged by the national government—has prepared an aggressive plan for restructuring the city in a polynucleated pattern, with a grid of infrastructure that equalizes access and service across the urbanizing area. A public development entity has been created to take the lead in carrying out key projects that promote this agenda. In the metropolitan Toronto area, the governmental structure has been changed three times since the 1960's, extending powers of the metropolitan government further outward; recently, the powers were devolved when it was judged that Metro Toronto had become too large to manage as a single governmental entity.

In the United States there is no need to promote more decentralization, which is still being advocated for some European and Asian cities. Quite the opposite, most politicians and planners are interested in achieving greater densities and less spread. In Tokyo, the metropolitan region in 1960 was not nearly as dense as it is today; it was largely a low-rise city with a fine-grained mixture of commerce and housing. But a combination of public and private bodies have built fifteen new rapid-transit lines since World War II, adding to a transit system that was already quite good. That investment in infrastructure plus extraordinarily tight controls on the urbanization of farmlands has limited the spread of development and promoted infilling and much greater densities. Tokyo is now a region of 32 million residents that works more effectively than cities a fraction of its size.

Through a combination of public and private investment, a series of new subcenters has been built in Tokyo over the past two decades. They are located in two rings: a set of new "downtowns" in the inner city, connected by the Yamanote JR line, built around the terminals of commuter rail lines, and forming a ring about 5 miles around the Imperial Palace; and an outer ring, 20–30 miles from central Tokyo. Each subcenter is served by mass transit, commuter rail, and expressways, and infrastructure continues to be developed to expand access between the centers. Each of the outlying centers has a distinct character and mix of functions: MM21 in Yokohama is centered on tourism and conventions; Tokyo Teleport in the harbor is the center for media; Makuhari Messe, halfway between Tokyo and Narita, provides the region's largest exposition center and is a place for international businesses; Tskuba Science City focuses on higher education and research, and so on. All of the areas contain housing, cultural facilities, and entertainment, as well as employment, so that it is possible to live and work in close proximity. With these, and many other efforts aimed at improving the quality of life, Tokyo is today a multicentered and highly livable regional city covering several hundred square miles.

Planning for the New Realities in the United States

American cities are unlikely to muster the will to emulate Tokyo, but one of the important lessons to be learned from Tokyo is the necessity of having a regional development strategy. Following from this is the need for some entity to promote the regional agenda; it cannot be left to local municipalities. Part of the difficulty of creating and maintaining a regional agenda is the common perception that central cities and their surrounding areas are in competition with each other. Each time an expanding business relocates from a central area to the perimeter, the sense of competition is reinforced. Certainly central cities have had to bear a disproportionate burden of the costs of metropolitan development and are faced with large populations in need of public assistance and services. Absent significant state aid, they have been forced to tax at rates that discourage new businesses from locating there, further exacerbating their problems. As David Rusk first noted, elastic cities—those able to expand their boundaries to capture new residents and tax revenues—have fared better across many dimensions of metropolitan success. Put differently, recognizing interdependence allows urban regions to organize more effectively to be competitive, functioning regional areas.

Every Metropolitan Region Needs a Regional Development Strategy and a Permanent Mechanism for Promoting It

Books and articles advising every metropolitan region to emulate Portland, Oregon, have worn out their welcome. Certainly this is a good course of action if local politics permit. However, there is a need for alternatives.

One alternative is a private, advisory group. The Regional Plan Association (RPA) of New York and New Jersey has published three influential plans over the past seventy-five years and has had a surprising degree of influence by simply filling the vacuum and framing the discourse about the New York–centered region. Its first plan, in 1929, helped shape the program of building the area's first expressways and provided an agenda for acquiring open spaces and creating recreation areas. In 1968, the second regional plan emphasized building up secondary regional centers in downtown Brooklyn, the Jamaica area of Queens, White Plains in Westchester, Stamford in Southern Connecticut, and Newark, New Jersey, where strong transportation links justified more intense development. Many of these have evolved into new regional subcenters. The RPA's recent third regional plan, A Region at Risk, advocates renewing the regional infrastructure, creating better suburb to suburb links, and creating town centers in areas where older shopping centers will be redeveloped. RPA has no formal authority; it must rely on public persuasion and its influential board of directors to see its intentions realized.

Another example of an advisory regional plan is Chicago Metropolis 2020, recently prepared by the Commercial Club of Chicago in association with the American Academy of Arts and Sciences. EcoCity Cleveland has rethought its regions in terms of the preservation of natural systems. The advantage of regional plans generated by private organizations is that they are relatively easy to start and nobody has to agree to their creation. The disadvantage is that there is no enforcement mechanism.

Some citizen-based initiatives such as 1000 Friends of Oregon and Save the Bay have achieved results that transcend local boundaries by focusing on a narrow set of purposes—stopping land filling of San Francisco Bay and opening its edges to the public, and promoting compact, transit-centered development at the edges of Portland, in these two cases. But other such interest groups have also made it extraordinarily difficult and time-consuming to construct region-shaping infrastructure, such as new airports, expressways, and transit lines, and there is a need for a coalition of interests for such projects.

Efforts in the United States to adjust governmental boundaries to match regional realities have been largely unsuccessful, except in those areas where annexation allows city governments to expand their boundaries outward. Despite the rhetoric of states' rights and the clear constitutional responsibility of states for their local governments, local politics, racial and class differences, and strong traditions of home rule create an impasse where even tinkering with revenues and responsibilities is difficult. However, there is one regional governmental institution, the metropolitan planning organization (MPO) in every metropolitan area. Under federal law the transportation priorities for a region have to be set by the MPO. Many of these organizations are merely forums for negotiation among the local governments that are represented. But a few, such as the Association of Bay Area Governments around San Francisco and the San Diego Association of Governments, have produced regional plans as a context for their regional transportation priorities. Outside of transportation, however, such a plan is, again, purely advisory. Charlotte-Mecklenburg is a city–county government that was meant to be a regional government; but urban sprawl has continued beyond the county boundaries. However, the Charlotte-Mecklenburg Planning Commission has organized a series of regional planning initiatives, including a recent "audit" of urban sprawl, which included an alternative vision of the region as a series of centers linked by transportation corridors.

It is often easier to create new governmental entities for special purposes than to modify those that exist. Regional authorities have been established to create, finance, and operate metropolitan infrastructure, such as transit, ports, airports, expressways, and sewer and water systems, but rarely have these been coupled with effective regional planning efforts. The new Georgia Regional Transportation Authority may prove to be an exception.

One possibility for effective regional policies would be the creation of a regional development district, with responsibility for growth centers and major infrastructure projects, coupled with the capacity to lead a process of visioning and debating regional opportunities. Much of the extraordinary costs of infrastructure in growth areas might be recouped through taxes on increased land values. In Japan, incremental land values around transit stations are frequently captured or taxed to pay for the transit facilities themselves. Examples of effective mechanisms for regional action exist in many places in the United States—regional service districts in Boston and Atlanta; urban development corporations in New York State; business improvement districts with bonding capacity, as in New York and Philadelphia; and tax increment districts found in many states. It remains to put these mechanisms together into an effective and coordinated capacity to pursue regional development. A further complexity is that many metropolitan regions cross state lines. But there are a number of models of bi-state authorities that have been effective, including the Port Authority of New York and New Jersey, which has served as a capable advocate for economic development of the region as well as an operator of key transportation facilities.

More Power and Responsibility Need to Devolve to Local Governments

At the same time that greater regional capacity is needed, many of the functions operated at the scale of counties or big municipalities could benefit by devolution to smaller entities. Housing improvement programs could be more effective if carried out by neighborhood-based entities. Local zoning decisions are most effectively administered by bodies elected on a neighborhood level, who are sensitive to local needs and aspirations. Here the differentiation between areas of the city that are of regional importance (large commercial and office districts, industrial areas, ports, and other regional facilities, and so on) from local areas is critical. Current charter proposals in Los Angeles advocate devolution of many zoning functions to local councils. Many municipal services are also better administered on a small area basis, as New York's creation of community service districts—which correspond to community planning boards—has demonstrated. Charter schools offer an important alternative to the monopoly of school boards in public education. The objective of all of these moves should be to allow genuine differentiation of the quality of environment and services across the metropolitan region. Regions such as Massachusetts Bay, which have a long tradition of localism, demonstrate the virtues of such differences.

Planning Is a Necessity for Successful Cities and Regions

If the past century of development leaves any lesson, it is that the detailed relationships, even design, of urban areas ultimately affects their desirability and attractiveness. Suburban clusters fall far short of their potentials precisely because they lack the planning for ways that pedestrians move from place to place, have a poor mix of facilities, waste land for under-used parking areas, and lack access alternatives. It is not accidental that many of the most desirable urban areas are cities with active planning efforts. Improving the parts of the city that have declined or have evolved in haphazard ways will require more, not less, planning. Locality and region are the dual necessities of every urban resident. The next century will require a policy framework that recognizes these as critical aspects of modern life and that creates an accommodation between them.

Recommendations

1. Every metropolitan region needs a regional plan.
Whether it is produced by a private organization, an MPO, or an alliance of planning commissions, it is necessary to lay out regional alternatives and issues so that everyone can see and understand them. Eventually every region will need an effective regional government, or at least a group of regional implementing agencies, but just the existence of a regional plan is a major step forward.

2. Every city and county has to give more decision-making power to local districts.
As metropolitan regions grow in size, effective power over decisions can become remote from individual citizens. Local neighborhoods and districts need to keep control over their futures, so the increase in planning and governmental power for regions has to be balanced by more neighborhood control over matters, like planning, where local citizens have the best insights.

P A R T   2

Managing Growth and Conserving the Environment

Chapter 3
Social Equity and Metropolitan Growth

John C. Keene

As we stand at the threshold of the twenty-first century, there are a number of questions that we must answer about the development patterns and growth processes of our metropolitan areas:

1. Should we continue the current policies that encourage middle and upper middle class families to move from cities to suburbs and leave economically immobile, low- and moderate-income families trapped in places with declining economies? Should we keep building new infrastructure on the fringes of our metropolitan areas that duplicates the existing, underused infrastructure in the central cities? Or should we find ways to limit the spread of urbanization, redirect development back toward bypassed areas of older cities and suburbs, limit the influence of race as a measure of participation in the American dream, and stimulate new employment and the creation of desirable communities where people of the middle and upper middle class would like to come and live?

2. Should we continue to encourage construction of single-family detached housing developments that no longer meet the needs of a majority of the nation's households, whose demographic characteris-

tics have changed in the past fifty years? Or should we adopt policies that assure the construction of a range of housing types that more closely meet the needs of our changing population: town houses, multifamily housing, and mobile homes?

3. Should we continue to construct our metropolitan areas so that the automobile is the principal means of transportation, or should we seek ways of reducing automobile usage with its attendant congestion, air pollution, and consumption of imported oil products, by making it easier to walk and use bicycles and mass transit—in short, to promote more sustainable cities?

4. Should we continue to build power generation plants, trash-to-steam plants, and other locally unwanted land uses disproportionately near areas where low and moderate-income families or minority families live? Or should we actively pursue more environmentally equitable policies at all levels of government?

5. Should we continue to encourage the unnecessary conversion of hundreds of thousands of acres of farmland, following the practices of the past several decades? Or should we find ways of maintaining the agricultural economy, making it possible for farmers to keep farming and make a decent living and also to reduce some of the incentives they have to sell to a developer, thus protecting farming communities, farming economies, and farmland?

6. Finally, should we continue federal and state policies that deter potential buyers from purchasing and redeveloping any of the hundreds of thousands of vacant urban properties in the United States by exposing them to strict, retroactive liability for the cost of remediating past ground and water pollution? Or should we try to find ways of making it easier and more attractive for commercial real estate to acquire these properties, find out what is wrong with them, and remediate them without being exposed to potential clean-up liabilities that may total millions of dollars?

Consequences of Urban Sprawl

Under our federal system, the primary responsibility for guiding urban development and redevelopment rests at the state and local level, although it is clear that federal programs such as the interstate highway program,

Federal Housing Administration (FHA) mortgage insurance, Department of Veterans Affairs (VA) mortgage guarantees, and grant-in-aid programs for sewerage systems and waste water treatment plants have influenced the patterns of growth and facilitated development in areas where it would not otherwise have taken place.

The process of urban development that we have experienced in the past forty years cannot be sustained indefinitely, and we may already be reaching its limits. It rests on extravagant rates of land consumption—in metropolitan area after metropolitan area, the rate at which land is consumed by new subdivisions vastly exceeds the rate at which the number of households is increasing. The exponentially increasing rate of consumption of energy for auto transportation, air conditioning, packaging, use of electrical appliances, means only that the day of reckoning when the supply of fuel is insufficient to meet the need will arrive sooner rather than later. Other nonrenewable resources, such as good farmland, are also being consumed at a profligate rate. In addition, there are large social and financial penalties.

Suburban governments have had to build whole new physical and social infrastructural systems (transportation facilities, water and sewer systems, sewage treatment plants, schools, police departments, etc.), often with substantial subsidies from the federal government, while older cities have experienced over-capacity and under-usage.

Many of those who were left behind in the central cities have not been able to obtain the proper education or appropriate employment that would allow them to put their abilities to productive use.

Policies of the Home Owners Loan Corporation and the FHA in the 1930s and 1940s (also adopted by the VA) effectively red-lined urban areas where African Americans and low income families lived, making them ineligible for federal mortgage insurance and guarantees. One result was to induce white families to move to newer suburban areas, leaving African Americans behind in the old cities. The FHA's policies also favored the construction of single-family residences over multifamily units. In fact, the FHA encouraged the use of racially restrictive covenants until 1950. As one analyst put it, the national government "put its seal of approval on ethnic and racial discrimination and developed policies that had the result of practical abandonment of large sections of older, industrial cities."[1]

As new communities were built on the urban fringe, they covered over irreplaceable farmland and other lands of high resource value. Farm economies were disrupted as land values rose, making it impossible for new farmers to begin to farm, and intruding suburbanites began to complain about the odors, the dust, the pesticides and fertilizer, and the other externalities of agricultural production.

Too often, the housing that was built in the exurbs was unsuited to the needs of the smaller families, often headed by a single mother or childless, that constituted most of the home-buying public of the late twentieth century.

America's love affair with the automobile, the declining real cost of gasoline, and the distributed, unfocused pattern of suburban development meant that the car was, of necessity, the mode of transportation. The result was a decline in community life, increasing road congestion and decreasing mass transit ridership, and higher levels of air pollution, especially by car-generated ozone, oxides of nitrogen, and particulate matter.

Too often, necessary but undesirable facilities such as sewage treatment plants, trash-to-steam plants, recycling facilities, landfills, and heavy manufacturing plants were located near minority or poor communities. The result was that families in these areas, who were often least able to exercise political influence to block the location of such facilities near them, were forced to add environmental pollution to the burdens that they were already enduring

Substantial barriers stood in the way of a sensible redevelopment effort that would redirect current centrifugal development pressures back to the center of our major metropolitan areas: poor schools, high real or perceived rates of crime, environmental pollution from abandoned industrial and commercial sites, and centuries-old prejudices that militated against social integration across racial or cultural lines.

In many parts of the country, especially New England, the Mid-Atlantic, and the Midwest, local governmental structure was fractionated and Balkanized. Since this is the level at which land development and redevelopment are most often regulated, it has meant that the policies that motivated these processes were parochial and informed by the values of a small and unrepresentative part of the total population. The span of local government control and the range of values it promoted were much narrower than the scale of the economic and social phenomena that drove urban development.

Clearly, the factors that have contributed to urban sprawl are deeply rooted in the American psyche, our moral values and biases, and the nation's governmental and economic systems. To modify these forces will require fundamental changes in the way we manage urban development and redevelopment. As difficult as this may seem, this is what is happening in community after community and state after state around the country. Most of these innovations have occurred—and must occur—at the state and local level because this is where the principal locus of land use control lies.

State and Local Policies and Programs for Combating Urban Sprawl

Fourteen states now have growth management legislation. The first states to adopt such laws were Hawaii in 1961, Vermont in 1970 (amended in 1987), and Florida in 1972 (amended in 1985). Oregon passed its Land Use Law in 1973. New Jersey is next in 1985 (amended in 1992). In 1988, Maine and Rhode Island both adopted comprehensive growth management programs, followed by Georgia in 1989. Washington State's growth management laws date from 1990 and 1991. Maryland adopted growth management laws in 1992 and amended them substantially in 1997. South Carolina followed suit in 1994, Minnesota in 1997, Tennessee in 1998, and Pennsylvania adopted "Growing Smarter" legislation in 2000. Other states, like Utah, have adopted advisory procedures that go some of the way toward growth management. As state legislation is necessary to manage metropolitan growth, techniques that have won political acceptance in some states may eventually find acceptance in many other states.

Hawaii adopted statewide zoning, the only state that has kept direct control over development. All the others have delegated zoning power to local governments. Hawaii's objective was to protect resort areas and local farmland by establishing strong controls in some districts and encouraging development in others. Vermont, although a politically conservative state, was motivated to protect its scenic resources and its quality of life against growing pressures from developers of tourist facilities, by enacting growth management legislation that retrieved some of the power that had been delegated to local governments and creating a level of regional agencies with important responsibilities over major developments.

Florida responded to tremendous growth pressures that began in the 1960s by building a comprehensive planning and growth management process that includes local plans, regional plans, and a statewide coordinating process. Enacted first in 1972, it was amended substantially in 1985. Florida was the first state to deal specifically with infrastructure issues by establishing the principle of "concurrency": that development should not go forward without reliable assurance that the necessary infrastructure will be built to support it. Florida has also enacted a number of other laws designed to protect the natural environment, including the coastal environment and the Everglades.

Oregon was the first state to require each metropolitan area to set specific urban growth boundaries, delineating an area around a city or a town where new development over the next twenty years should take place. Publicly financed infrastructure to support development is to be constructed inside the boundary, but not outside. Created primarily to protect farmland, urban growth boundaries, supplemented by other policies, have proved to be a powerful metropolitan planing tool. The Portland Metropolitan Service District is an actual regional government, one of the few in the United States. It has adopted a regional plan that will accommodate predicted population growth primarily by intensifying development along rapid transit lines, rather than by expanding the growth boundary, which has been enlarged by only 7 percent. Portland's policies are already producing substantial reinvestment in older areas where infrastructure already exists, as well as limiting new infrastructure investments outside the growth boundary.

Constructing highways opens new areas to development, and constructing sewage treatment plants and public water supply systems enables high-density development to take place in newly accessible areas. This development then has to be supported by schools, fire and police services, and other local facilities. When a state funds new infrastructure in rural areas, it is pursuing a de facto policy of decanting population out of older cities and towns. Georgia and New Jersey have been experimenting with state planning policies to control the effects of these expenditures but the most comprehensive approach has been Maryland's.

Maryland, still a significant agricultural state but under tremendous development pressure, especially in the eastern half of the state, adopted the Economic Growth, Resource Protection and Planning Act in 1992. The act recognizes that economic growth is desirable, but that protecting farmland and the economies of existing cities and towns is equally important. The 1997 amendments created the "Smart Growth" program that made financial incentives available to counties and local governments that participated in effective comprehensive planning. The most important aspect of the act is that it recognizes the role that state funding plays in opening up new areas to development. It gives priority to infrastructure projects that will reinforce existing population centers and will be consistent with growth management plans. There are also programs to encourage reinvestment in older urban areas.

Farmland Protection

Not every metropolitan area is a candidate for a farmland protection program because not every metropolitan area has a lot of good farmland. But there are many metropolitan areas that do. The area to the west of the East Coast megalopolis, running from New York down through Pennsylvania, Maryland, and into Virginia has some of the most productive farmland close to the cities. The American Farmland Trust has identified the area as one of those that is under heavy development pressure from urban sprawl. Washington State is a major producer of apples and other fruit, and orchards are under development pressure from Seattle and other major cities. Another seriously threatened area is the Central Valley in California east of San Francisco and to the north and south between the mountain ranges. It is the richest agricultural production area in the country but is under serious development pressure. Land values are going up, and the fear is that much land will be converted in the next decade or two. California is the biggest agricultural state in the United States, and the Central Valley is its main resource. Farmland cannot be replaced after it has been developed, and good farmland with low transportation costs to cities is especially valuable. It makes sense to try to protect it.

The challenge in farmland protection is to create an integrated program that uses the major techniques that are available: agricultural zoning, differential assessment of farmland, purchase of agricultural easements, agricultural district programs, transferable development rights, right to farm laws, and control over growth-inducing, state supported infrastructural investments and policies, agricultural economic development programs, and general growth management programs in ways that are suited to the economic and political conditions in a particular jurisdiction. State legislatures should support state efforts to protect the agricultural economy and assure that local governments are authorized to create the kinds of programs they need to achieve this goal.

Of course, it is also important to take steps to promote the agricultural economy and to get state growth management in place. Saving farmland is not of much use unless farmers have an economic incentive to continue, and growth management is needed to deflect development from prime farming areas.

If land is already zoned for uses other than agriculture and is already under development pressure, it is possible to purchase agricultural conservation easements (PACE). Eighteen states have programs to purchase agricultural conservation easements. The state pays the farmer the difference between the fair market value of the land subjected to the easement and the farm use value for the right to prevent all development except that permitted by the easement. This can be an expensive purchase: thousands of dollar per acre or, in some cases, tens of thousands per acre. As of June 1999, over 565,000 acres of farmland in 3,625 properties had been protected in this way under state programs at a cost of approximately $850 million. Many counties and municipalities have also adopted PACE programs. As of February 1999, some thirty-four such programs in eleven states have protected at least 150,000 acres on 1,100 farms at a cost of over $260 million.

Development pressures raise property values. When land values go up, property taxes go up. If a farmer is making only $100 to $150 per acre, a tax of $30 per acre will consume all of his profit. All but two states have adopted differential assessment programs that reduce the assessed value of eligible farms to the agricultural-use value, and thereby keep taxes low. The remaining two states have what are known as "circuit- breaker" programs that achieve the same result. Property tax incentives that cap the amounts that farmers have to pay are critically important, but without integrated growth management, agricultural zoning, and development-rights purchases, they will seldom be sufficient to slow the conversion of farmland in rapidly growing metropolitan areas.

Protecting Other Natural Resource Areas

Several states have created special purpose agencies to protect areas of scenic and ecological importance that are not in coastal zones. Created in 1971, New York's Adirondacks Park Development Commission extended strong protections to the natural resources in that 6 million acre area in the center of New York state. A special bi-state compact between California and Arizona regulates and limits development around Lake Tahoe. The Martha's Vineyard Commission, created in 1974, seeks to protect the qualities that make the island a major resort destination. The New Jersey Pinelands Commission was created in 1979 to protect a fragile resource—the roughly 1 million acre Pinelands, characterized by fragile marsh and lowland wooded areas—from the development pressures of the East Coast megalopolis. The Pineland Commission has substantial authority over comprehensive planning and zoning in the fifty-three municipalities that have territory within the Pinelands area, and it has been able to guide almost all of the new development in the region into specially designated growth areas and away from environmentally fragile marshes, woodlands, and agricultural areas.

Brownfields Remediation

For centuries, industrialists in the United States did not have to worry about hazardous waste; they could just dump it, as there were only poorly articulated, weakly enforced common-law doctrines concerning solid waste disposal. Our capacity to generate hazardous and toxic waste has increased enormously, and the wastes are much more dangerous. And for a long time manufacturers simply disposed of wastes as inexpensively as possible, often by simply storing them on site in drums that soon corroded and spilled their contents into the environment. In 1980 Congress enacted the Superfund law (the Comprehensive Environmental Response, Compensation and Liability Act), which required the U.S. Environmental Protection Agency to identify the worst, most dangerously polluted industrial sites. These were placed on a National Priorities List, and money was made available to remediate them. This law also imposed liability for clean-up costs on a number of private parties: those who generated the waste in the first place, those who shipped the waste to the site, and those who owned the site or building at the time the waste was deposited or at any time thereafter. Each could be liable for the complete cost of remediating these Superfund sites. The average Superfund site costs $32,000,000 to remediate. There are about 1,400 of these worst-case Superfund sites, many of which have been cleaned up (676 as of January 2000). Shortly after Congress enacted the Superfund law, some forty-six states also passed laws that created the same kind of liability at the state level for less seriously polluted properties.

The result of the passage of these federal and state laws is that no sensible businessperson wants to buy these properties, for fear of becoming liable for substantial clean-up costs, even if the purchaser had nothing to do with creating the problem in the first place. If a preliminary engineering check fails to identify a hazardous waste location, the owner could be required to pay millions of dollars in remediation expenses, which would destroy the profitability and attractiveness of the site. In an effort to address these concerns, Congress has funded a special "Brownfield Pilot Project Grant Program" under which the U.S. Environmental Protection Agency has awarded funds to over 300 pilot programs designed to encourage remediation of brownfields, including Assessment Demonstration, Revolving Loan Fund, Job Training and Development, and Demonstration Showcase Community Pilots. These projects are intended to stimulate innovation in site assessment methods, reduction of uncertainty as to liability for clean-up costs, greater participation by community groups in reuse planning for brownfields, and local job development and training initiatives. Congress also created a special tax incentive in 1997 that permitted developers of brownfield sites in economically depressed areas to deduct the cost of remediation as an ordinary business expense, rather than having to add it to the cost basis of their property. The EPA estimated that this decrease in the after-tax cost of site remediation might stimulate up to $5 or $6 billion in revitalization and return as many as 14,000 properties to economically productive use. In fact, the EPA's total budget for brownfield remediation for each of the fiscal years 1999 and 2000 is about $90 million.

Most of the states have been trying to deal with this issue by writing new laws. Pennsylvania enacted its Land Recycling Laws in 1995, which are among the best in the country. They make it easier for an industrial developer to buy one of these sites by limiting the risk. They require planning studies of how such properties ought to be used in the future, given that land use affects the amount of remediation required. They also protect lenders. Banks have been wary of financing the purchase of formerly industrial properties because, if a borrower defaults and the bank is forced to step in and manage the site, it might be liable for cleaning it up.

Originally, remediation standards for hazardous wastes contemplated restoring all land virtually to the way it was before any development took place. We now realize this may be an unnecessarily high standard, which can prevent remediation from taking place at all. For example, if land is to continue in industrial uses, it does not need the same level of expense for remediation required for residential uses, where children might be outside in the yard, playing in the dirt.

Protecting new owners from liability, creating financial support for remediation, and relating remediation standards to land uses could unlock the development potential of large areas of formerly industrial land in older cities and towns. Development of these areas, many of which are potentially attractive waterfront sites that are well located in relation to regional transportation and have many utilities in place, will help these older areas compete with metropolitan fringe locations—the so-called greenfield sites—for new development.

Disproportionately Low Density and Automobile Primacy

The disproportionately low densities found in many newly urbanized areas and their heavy dependence on automobile transportation are interrelated issues. The automobile is a wonderfully flexible mode of transportation, but land-use plans based on automobile access have little structure: extensive areas of large-lot zoning, long, undifferentiated commercial corridors. But metropolitan planning requires structure, which means that local planning authorities have to make decisions about where development should be dense enough to support public transportation and where development should not happen at all.

Environmental Justice

Since as long ago as the 1960s, federal and state programs have been scrutinized to determine the extent to which they imposed burdens disproportionately on economically disadvantaged and minority communities. For instance, many characterized the 1949 Housing Act's Urban Renewal

Program as a "Negro Removal Program," because it had the effect of demolishing homes in those "blighted" parts of our cities where the poor and a disproportionate number of minority families lived, in pursuit of the goal of urban redevelopment, often for housing for middle- and upper-middle-class families. Site selection processes for the interstate highway program and for unwanted land uses such as electrical power plants, trash-to-steam facilities, land-fills, and major heavy industrial plants, often located these facilities near disadvantaged communities. Usually, the reason was that the land was cheaper, or that the area was already an industrial area so that it made good sense to locate more manufacturing plants there. Critics charged that even if these decisions were not driven by overtly racist attitudes, they amounted to a form of institutional racism in that, too often, they imposed excessive burdens on minority and poor communities. As the years passed, the nature of the criticism shifted to an emphasis on environmental equity. Environmental policies should be implemented, so it was argued, in ways that imposed external costs of new facilities or conferred the benefits of environmental remediation on all sectors of society proportionally, or equitably. The concept of environmental justice is broader. It seeks to link social and environmental policies that will improve the quality of life for all members. Recent United Nations conferences have reflected a growing consensus that environmental problems resulting from excessive population growth in developing countries can only be solved by the institution of policies that, among other things, promote the education of women and the enhancement of their independence and income-producing capacity. The gist of the concept is to move toward a just society, one that distributes environmental costs and benefits fairly, as well as social and economic costs and benefits.

The principles of environmental justice bear equally on metropolitan development. The issue may be the siting of land uses that have negative effects on nearby neighborhoods, such as power stations or landfills. It may be combating the excesses of suburban exclusionary zoning that keep out most middle and low income families because they are disproportionately minority, or because they will need more municipal services than the property tax revenues from their new homes will support. In any case, the principles of environmental justice are as important for metropolitan development strategies as for national or international policies.

Recommendations

1. Limit growth at the metropolitan fringe.

A diverse enough group of states has now passed growth management legislation to show that it is possible for all states to do so in time. To accelerate the process, Congress could make some kinds of federal aid conditional on states having growth management legislation. Putting such a condition on highway funds would be very effective.

Congress could also place conditions on other infrastructure grant-in-aid programs that would work as levers to favor redevelopment of older cities and slow the movement to the periphery.

2. Encourage a mix of housing types.

Developers would be able to adjust more readily to changing housing market conditions if local codes permitted a greater mixture of housing types and sizes. This is primarily a zoning issue, and there is an extended treatment of it in Chapter 4.

3. Use taxes to increase the relative cost of automobile transportation.

The obvious candidate is an increase in the federal gasoline tax with the money going into a rapid transit trust fund. The political problems with this idea are equally obvious, but as it becomes increasingly clear that automobile transportation by itself cannot support current development, the politics will change. States can also use gasoline taxes to create rapid transit trust funds.

4. Promote environmental justice.

Make sure that the site selection criteria for all federally funded projects with adverse impacts include an evaluation of the past history of a site and an evaluation of whether the area has been burdened with a disproportionate number of such projects in the past. State and local site selection processes should use similar criteria. Review the impacts of federal antipollution laws, such as the Clean Water Act and the Clean Air Act that, in the name of reducing or preventing environmental pollution, have disproportionate impacts on older urban areas. For instance the Clean Air Act's limitations on the construction of new industrial facilities on sites that are in serious nonattainment of ozone ambient air quality standards can deter needed economic development in older cities. The Clean Water Act's total maximum daily load limitation for urban rivers may also inhibit desirable urban revitalization. The challenge is to prevent industrial development in areas where new jobs are badly needed from being penalized by the problems created by faulty development policies elsewhere in the metropolitan region.

5. Create comprehensive farmland protection programs.

Make sure that state enabling legislation permits agricultural zoning. There is no point in creating development rights that in turn create development pressures. Tax assessments of agricultural land can then be based on its agricultural value. Where necessary, there should be trust funds for the purchase of agricultural easements. Other measures include agricultural district programs, right to farm laws, and state executive orders that require state agencies to factor farmland protection into their functional programs

6. Encourage inner city revitalization.

Continue using tax incentives and deregulation to encourage urban revitalization, such as enterprise zones and empowerment zones. Remove or reduce the legal liability hurdles to the remediation of the hundreds of thousands of "brownfields." Relate clean-up standards to projected land uses. Create grants for riverfront restoration and other open space development to make older urban areas more competitive with suburbs. Make grants for stormwater treatment by natural systems, creating urban open space instead of costly treatment plants—see the discussion of this issue in Chapter 11.

NOTE

1. Kenneth Jackson, *Crabgrass Frontier* (New York: Oxford University Press, 1985), 217.

Chapter 4

Regional Design: Local Codes as Cause and Cure of Sprawl

Jonathan Barnett

Individual citizens and local governments have much more control over the design of their communities than most people believe. Discussions about sustainable environments include worldwide population and global pollution issues, but a big piece of the sustainability issue is the destruction of the natural landscape by individual development projects as cities and towns expand. "Smart growth" is a term that includes many of the issues discussed in this book, but a lot of the projects that are the opposite of smart growth are approved by local planning and zoning boards. The phrase "livable communities" is used to describe neighborhoods that contain a mix of different kinds of houses and apartments in addition to parks, a neighborhood school, and local shops, all in close enough proximity that people can walk to some of their destinations. Local governments that want to consider this alternative to conventional subdivision development have the power to do so.

Most local land use regulation in the United States is based on prototype-enabling legislation published by the U.S. Department of Commerce in the 1920s under Secretary Herbert Hoover. Although modern zoning and subdivision codes have evolved from these early models, they do not deal effectively with office parks and big-scale housing developments, or with large and complex building types like regional shopping centers that did not exist in the 1920s. While every new project must be approved under local law, these laws often produce results that neither the public nor the development industry really wants. Much of the recipe for urban sprawl can be found in local zoning and subdivision regulations. The endless ribbons of commercial development along highways all follow zoning; so do the big tracts of suburban houses, each the same size on the same sized lots. The drastic stripping and bulldozing of the suburban landscape often result from the requirements in the subdivision ordinance.

Even where state growth management legislation requires local government to draw growth boundaries, as in Oregon, the development within the boundary is likely to follow the familiar sprawl patterns under the dead hand of outmoded development regulation.

The American Planning Association is currently developing a *Growing Smart Legislative Guidebook* that will help states revise their enabling legislation. Eventually the innovations in the guidebook will filter down to local governments. However, it is possible to correct many of the imperfections in local land-use legislation without waiting for a comprehensive review of state enabling legislation.

Recognizing Land as Landscape

The biggest weakness in current zoning and subdivision laws is that they treat land as a commodity and not an ecosystem.

Zoning determines how much development may go on a given piece of land and what activities will be permitted. As far as zoning laws are concerned, the landscape might as well be a Monopoly board or a billiard table. In fact the billiard table is sometimes referred to as the platonic ideal of landscape when practitioners are trying to determine how many lots and houses should fit on a given site.

Subdivision ordinances set the rules for laying out streets and dividing large tracts of land into individual building lots. These ordinances do recognize that land has contours, by setting a maximum gradient for streets. This regulation changes the land into something as much like a Monopoly board as possible. If all streets in a subdivision may not slope at a grade of more than 5 percent, and the site is divided up by a conventional street system, the streets may ultimately be much more level than the rest of the land. Streets can end up on a berm, higher than the surrounding lots, or in a canyon between lots. If the streets are higher, the lawns and basements are likely to flood. If the streets are lower, they are a problem in wet weather. As neither alternative is desirable, and avoiding both is a complicated design problem, the developer is likely to bulldoze the high points of the landscape down into the low-lying areas and level the whole site. This kind of regrading means removing all the trees and other vegetation. It also means stripping the topsoil. What the builder eventually puts back in the way of soil and landscaping is often much less than what was there before; the house may be spacious and luxurious; but the treatment of the lot is skimped. Homeowners may discover that their lawn is turf laid down over subsoil, and their trees are really potted plants.

The individual homeowner's landscaping problems can be solved, although the cost may be an unpleasant surprise. The biggest problem with typical regrading practice is the cumulative effect on the regional ecosystem. Trees and shrubs retain rainwater, when they are removed the flow of water across the landscape is accelerated. Land contours have reached an equilibrium over time, when they are disturbed and then subjected to strong flows of water, erosion can take place with great rapidity.

An individual subdivision may have an internally consistent grading system, but what about its relationship with surrounding properties? Have they also been regraded? If not, there is likely to be an escarpment or a ditch at the property line, both unstable, erosion-prone conditions. If the neighboring property has also been regraded, the problems of accelerated run-off are likely to be multiplied. Many localities are discovering that floods of a magnitude that was once expected to occur every 100 or even 500 years are now a frequent occurrence.

Protecting the Environment by Planned Unit Development

The limitations of local zoning and subdivision codes have long been recognized, and most places have adopted a procedure called planned unit development to circumvent them. Just as the term suggests, streets, lots, and buildings are planned as a unit, and the plan becomes the zoning and subdivision for the property.

Under planned unit development, the usual procedure is to calculate the number of lots that would be attainable if the land were flat, the billiard table analogy. Under most planned unit development laws the local authorities have the discretion to approve any development plan that stays within the individual zoning envelope. The streets can also be nonstandard widths and have slopes greater than those normally permitted.

The discretion that is the strength of a planned unit development procedure is also its biggest weakness. As every element is negotiable, the planning authorities have to be able to distinguish between rigid, inappropriate controls and standards that need to be maintained. They don't always succeed. As the procedure is essentially a custom-tailored ordinance, there is also a temptation for the developer to ask for a zoning change along with the planned development, as each usually requires the same number of hearings and approvals. So, along with the plan approval may come a decision to permit a zoning calculation based on a higher zoning density. This may be a perfectly appropriate decision, but the density question gets entangled in the design and planning decisions, and it is difficult for the public to sort out their merits.

While one of the great advantages of planned unit development is that it facilitates leaving sensitive natural landscapes undisturbed, this is not always the result. The erosion and other environmental damage caused by a planned unit development can be as severe as that caused by a conventional plan.

Other Methods for Protecting the Environment

As the subdivision ordinance is the part of local development regulation that controls the specifics of land planning, adding environmental provisions can make it more effective in protecting the local ecology. The subdivision ordinance can specify that there should be no changes to natural drainageways and steep hillsides, and it can require the developer to show how buildings will be kept away from sink holes, sites of previous landslides, or any flood plains and wetlands. There can also be restrictions for places with easily erodible soils or land formations susceptible to erosion.

In addition, there can be water-retention requirements that say that water should leave the property no faster after development than it did before. If this goal cannot be attained by conservation measures, it is possible to channel run-off water into detention ponds.

Putting such specific requirements into the subdivision ordinance makes it harder to waive them in a planned unit development, conversely meeting these requirements without a reduction in the permitted density probably requires planned unit development.

Environmental Zoning

In a planned unit development, why should density be calculated as if the land were a billiard table when it clearly is not? Shouldn't there be a reduction in the permitted development if the carrying capacity of the land doesn't support it? This is the issue raised by Lane Kendig in a book entitled *Performance Zoning* published in 1980. Kendig questioned the billiard-table theory of zoning entitlement. If a 100-acre parcel has only 70 acres of buildable land, why shouldn't the calculation of permitted development be based on the 70 acres? Why create development rights on unbuildable land, and then transfer them to the land that can be developed, causing it to be built on at a higher density than is specified in the zoning?

These are good questions. In most zoning ordinances, the area of land under development is the basis for calculating how much building is permitted. Kendig proposes a simple amendment to local zoning that discounts the land area for calculation purposes, based on the land's sensitivity to environmental damage. Land under water would be discounted 100 percent, hillsides above a certain steepness discounted 85 percent, lesser slopes a lesser percentage, and so on. There is no need for the local authority to map these areas itself. A map at 2-foot contours identifying any special-category land listed in the ordinance is provided by the developer as part of the application process.

This environmental zoning procedure clearly protects public safety, health, and welfare by reducing erosion and flooding. It is elegantly simple. It is objective. It applies uniformly to everyone. In other words it meets the constitutional tests for zoning. A local community can adopt it without any other changes in its zoning ordinance. Local communities can go a long way toward protecting the natural environment from the bad effects of future development by using environmental zoning in concert with planned unit development and specific environmental protection provisions in the subdivision ordinance.

Grading and Tree-Cutting Ordinances

What prevents a developer from stripping and bulldozing a property before applying for zoning and subdivision approval? Nothing, unless a community also has laws that require permits for grading and for cutting down trees larger than a specified size, usually a 6- or 8-inch caliper. The key phrase in such regulations is to require that grading or tree cutting be done in accordance with an approved development plan. Good draftsmanship can provide exceptions for working farms and for individual homeowners who want to do a small amount of tree cutting and clearing.

While environmental zoning and subdivision laws plus grading and tree-protection ordinances can protect a community against some of the damaging effects of sprawl, they can make other aspects of sprawl worse by thinning development and spreading it out over more of the natural landscape. Which brings us to the other major weakness of zoning, its lack of a positive template to shape development.

Making Zoning Positive as Well as Negative

Zoning began as a response to the intrusion of industry into cities and the invention of tall buildings. Zoning's original purpose was to separate incompatible activities, keeping residences away from the noisy and dirty factories, and protecting neighboring properties from big buildings that block all the light and air. The regulations were intended to guide changes and extensions to existing cities and towns, where districts and neighborhoods were already established and the general shape of development was already settled. No one anticipated that urbanization would spill out of cities and towns and cover whole metropolitan regions. Zoning has been the sole shaping force for most of this regional development and, while it still makes sense to separate heavy industry from residences and impose set-backs on towers, the over-all effect of zoning has been to make the metropolitan region far more fragmented and discontinuous than it needs or ought to be.

Zoning needs to be turned from a series of negative controls designed to protect the immediate neighbors of a development to a positive force that protects the whole community.

Problems with Current Land-Use Districts

What is called commercial-strip zoning is a good example of the inadequacy of current development regulations. When zoning was first invented, it made sense to map commercial frontages continuously along trolley-car streets in cities, or along the Main Street of a small town. It made a good deal less sense to apply the same zoning formula for miles along major arterial highways, beginning in the 1950s and 1960s; but it became an almost universal practice. There is too much commercial land along these continuous highway frontages for it to be used efficiently, and the commercial zone is too narrow for there to be an efficient cluster of development at any one place. The result is the familiar fragmented pattern of individual shops, restaurants, and small offices, each with its own sign and parking lot. The set-back and yard requirements in the zoning accentuate the discontinuity from one building to the next. Commercial strips are a big cause of the traffic tie-ups that plague suburbia. The arterial street itself becomes dysfunctional because of the people going in and out of business establishments, particularly if they are making left turns in the middle of the block. The separation of each building also generates more trips, as it is necessary to drive from destination to destination. The pattern is so ubiquitous that most people think it is the inevitable result of market forces, rather than the adaptation of the market to an outmoded zoning concept.

Zoning ordinances separate land uses. But cities and towns traditionally contained a mix of different activities. Most commercial zones permit a relatively wide range of uses, although they may not permit residences. Residential zones only allow residences. In addition, ordinances create a hierarchy of residential categories from single-family houses on large lots to apartment towers. Generally you can build a house in an apartment zone, although real estate economics make it unlikely, but you can't build an apartment building in a single-family house zone. There is some rational basis for this kind of segregation. An existing single-family house neighborhood that is rezoned to permit apartments may see a rash of small apartment buildings shoe-horned into residential lots. House values suffer and the apartments aren't much good either. But the idea that each gradation of housing density should be in a separate zone does not have much to do with separating incompatible land uses. It is a practice that grew up without sufficient consideration or evaluation.

Most neighborhoods begun before the 1950s contain a successful mix of lot sizes and building types, often within walking distance of neighborhood commercial centers. Newer suburban development is sharply differentiated by building type, reflecting the proliferation of zoning categories. There will be large areas of single-family homes on individual lots. The lots in each area will all be the same size, and so will the houses. Then there will be a section of garden apartments, but only garden apartments. There may be an enclave of townhouses. Here and there apartment towers are permitted. This kind of segregation no longer corresponds to social and economic categories, if it ever did. An elderly couple may prefer a condominium garden apartment to maintaining a house and yard, while still keeping up their country-club membership. But zoning forces them out of their old neighborhood into an apartment house zone, down by the railway tracks or next to the commercial district along the highway. Meanwhile, a young family with just one car can only find a rental townhouse miles away from the center of the community, out on the highway to the airport. The housing industry has been very successful in creating a variety of housing types, all with well-equipped kitchens, lavish bathrooms, and effective heating and cooling systems. Outmoded zoning patterns have made it much more difficult to create a similar variety and quality of neighborhoods. As fewer people belong to traditional families, a variety of housing types within the same community becomes more and more important, and the rigid residential segregation fostered by current zoning needs to be modified.

Improving Current Zoning

Communities can revise their zoning ordinances to shape development rather than just waiting to deal with development proposals as they come along. Zoning maps can be modified to enlarge commercial strips at key intersections into commercial mixed-use zones. These larger districts can become the equivalent of traditional town centers, where people can park once and walk between destinations. These districts can also become big enough to be served efficiently by buses or other types of public transit. Along the arterial highway, in between these enlarged commercial districts, the strip-commercial zoning can be phased out in favor of multifamily districts that permit a mixture of building types (Figure 4.1a, b, c,).

Communities can also add neighborhood zones to their ordinances; these zones permit a mix of residential building types and densities, as well as neighborhood stores (Figure 4.2a, b, c).

However, these kinds of zones won't shape development unless they can be backed by more specific plans that show how the stores and parking are laid out, or how the different neighborhood buildings relate to each

a

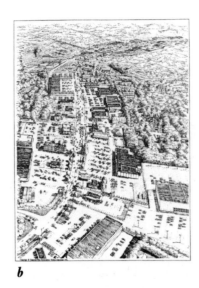

b

c

Figure 4.1. *a* These typical strips of commercial development along an arterial highway are built in response to the local zoning code. *b* If the zoning remains on the books, the development along the highway will intensify, creating more traffic congestion and an ugly and confused environment. *c* The zoning could be changed to development more like a town center at some locations along the strip, while intervening areas are rezoned for multifamily housing that relates to the surrounding neighborhoods. (Drawings used by permission of the Regional Plan Association. The collaborators on these drawings were Robert D. Yaro, Dodson Associates, and Jonathan Barnett.)

other. In areas that have not yet developed, if the commercial districts or neighborhood zones are all in one ownership, the community can use existing planned unit development regulations.

But what about areas that are already at least partially developed, or what about areas where ownership is divided?

In older cities, urban renewal regulations permit communities to

a

b

c

Figure 4.2. An agricultural landscape, *a*, is routinely transformed by large-lot zoning into tract development, *b*, where each house and lot is approximately the same size. While the individual houses are spacious, there is little sense of community and the character of the landscape is lost. *c* Alternative zoning codes permit development of neighborhoods, with a mix of house sizes, some apartments, a few convenience stores, and professional offices. As some of the development is at a higher density, part of the natural landscape can be saved, while housing the same number of people. (Drawings used by permission of the Regional Plan Association. The collaborators were Robert D. Yaro, Dodson Associates, and Jonathan Barnett.)

acquire land from various owners and reshape development. But the precondition for acquisition is that the land must be blighted. While the definition of "blight" is elastic, it may not apply in newer suburban areas. In any case, local communities do not usually have an urban renewal agency and don't want to undertake the costs and complications of property acquisition.

In California, communities can add specific plans to their zoning. These plans function like a planned unit development in that a specific design for streets and buildings replaces the usual zoning and subdivision regulations for the area covered by the plan, but the plans become binding on properties that belong to different owners. Oregon and Arizona have passed similar enabling legislation.

Some conventional planned unit development provisions may also be used to make decisions that are binding on multiple ownerships, depending on the wording of the state enabling legislation and the local zoning laws.

New York City has long used special zoning districts to cover areas in multiple ownership. Special districts are necessarily more abstract than planned unit developments or specific plans because they can't show actual architectural plans. Instead they rely on set-back and build-to lines to control building placement, and map features like arcades or interior pedestrian walkways as points that need to be connected, plus a specification of minimum dimensions.

Dade County in Florida has adopted a Traditional Neighborhood District as part of zoning, and similar legislation has also been adopted in other jurisdictions. The neighborhood is defined as an area no bigger than can be traversed in a ten-minute walk. Each neighborhood district permits a mix of different housing types and sets standards for building placement, public open space, and street layout. The legislation can also include typologies for street layouts and sections and for various types of building arrangements.

As zoning codes and subdivision regulations are jealously guarded local prerogatives, it is up to local communities to adopt environmental zoning and subdivision regulations. It is also up to local communities to adopt legislation to create neighborhood plans and specific plans for commercial districts.

Recommendations

1. Enact a grading and tree protection ordinance.
Grading and tree-cutting should not take place without a permit, and the permit should be conditioned on an approved development plan. Without this protection, other environmental protection legislation can be circumvented by site preparation before applications are made for development

approval. Agricultural activities and minor domestic changes in landscaping can be exempted in a well-drafted ordinance.

2. Enact environmental protection provisions.

Environmental protection provisions can be part of zoning or part of the subdivision ordinance. They should protect such areas as steep slopes, natural drainageways, and places with problem subsoil conditions to keep them from being disturbed during the development process. Planned unit development provisions will be needed so that the site plan can work around these areas. Some localities also reduce permitted densities by subtracting the most environmentally sensitive land from the density calculations.

3. Add a neighborhood category to the zoning ordinance.

A neighborhood zone permits a mix of different lot and house sizes and allows for civic buildings and a percentage of service commercial uses. It permits developers to propose communities instead of subdivisions.

4. Add specific plan districts to the zoning ordinance.

The specific plan procedure is similar in concept to planned unit development, but for areas in multiple ownership. The plan becomes the zoning for the area. Where enabling legislation permits, it can be made compulsory, otherwise the owners have to agree on the plan. This measure is particularly useful for replanning commercial districts.

In states that have environmental impact legislation, the community will have to review the environmental impact of such new zoning and subdivision provisions. This procedure has an advantage for developers. When the community has done the impact analysis at the "wholesale" level, individual developers who conform to the regulations of the district have no need to prepare their own environmental reviews.

Where the states can assist local communities is in making sure that enabling legislation permits environmental zoning and specific plans.

The federal government's role in land use is limited, but it could certainly help finance writing new legislation and preparing local plans. Grants for preparing environmental zoning and subdivision ordinances could be part of federal environmental protection programs. Preventing excessive water run-off in the first place is certainly more cost effective than building water-treatment plants to accommodate storm water. Federal transportation legislation could contain funds to encourage communities to plan compact commercial districts and mixed-density neighborhoods that could be served by public transportation.

Individual local codes, all derived from the same prototypes, have created similar development problems all across the United States. Individual local changes could also solve those problems.

Chapter 5

Next Steps in Controlling Pollution

Roger Raufer

Environmental pollution in urban areas is an old problem, and one that cities have been trying to deal with for a very long time. Smoke from coal combustion was a concern in early-fourteenth-century London, but even back then there were strong efforts to address the matter. An article in the *Cleveland State Law Review* notes that "in 1307 a Royal Proclamation was issued prohibiting the use of coal in furnaces. The following year a violator of the proclamation was executed for that offense."[1] Some doubt that any such execution ever took place (one historian suggests that this claim "invariably has no primary reference"),[2] but such an account nonetheless illustrates, in its starkest form, the nature of "command/control" regulation, which has been the principal paradigm for controlling pollution in the urban environment.

The most severe form of "command" is prohibition, still used today if the potential damage to the environment is severe, or if the problem is particularly egregious (e.g., we prohibit the use of polychlorinated biphenyls, or PCBs). Technology-based requirements—forcing firms to meet some emission limit or performance standard for their equipment—are now typically employed as the form of command. Monetary fines, or perhaps imprisonment for serious cases, are the new norms for "control."

One subsequent British command/control approach stipulated that facilities should be required to use the "best practicable means" of pollution control. If one put the best practicable means of pollution control technology on, say, a power plant, then whatever happened to the environment simply happened—after all, that emission source was doing the best that could be expected of it in terms of technology.

Such an approach to environmental protection was discussed in the United States in the 1960s, but an alternative was adopted instead. This alternative was based upon the idea that the truly important consideration was the quality of the environment itself, not the technology that could protect it. Environmental goals were thus developed in terms of environmental quality standards, and the technology-oriented requirements became recognized as the means to accomplish these goals. Expectations of what controls could accomplish were set through physical modeling. Figure 5.1 shows the resulting regulatory approach employed over the past several decades in the United States.

Today, however, two big changes are happening in environmental regulation. The first change addresses how we as a society set those environmental goals, and introduces the idea of environmental risk. The second change recognizes that governmental technology-oriented mandates are not always appropriate or sufficient, and that we must also harness economics to accomplish our environmental goals.[3]

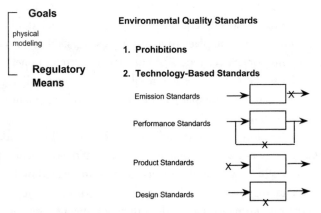

Figure 5.1. Command/control regulation. (Reprinted from Roger Raufer, *Pollution Markets in a Green Country Town* with permission of Praeger Publishers, Westport, Connecticut, 1998.)

Setting Environmental Goals

In the United States, we have set national ambient environmental standards that are applicable everywhere. We expect the air in Philadelphia to be as healthy as air in Kansas or Montana or at the Grand Canyon. We have special provisions to keep the air in pristine areas especially clean (i.e., PSD, or prevention of significant deterioration provisions), but the national goals are designed to achieve healthy air everywhere in the country.

What is the science behind these goals? Epidemiologists have performed statistical analyses that compare pollution levels and respiratory hospital visits and/or mortality, either in a single city over time or in different cities. Humans and animals have been exposed to various pollutant levels in special laboratory tests that measure physiological changes (e.g., a bicyclist's respiratory response will change when ozone levels are increased). Data are also available from industrial accidents where people have been exposed to high levels of pollutants over a short period of time. Some incidents of mass exposure to high levels of air pollution are also well known in the literature. Famous episodes of air pollution occurred in the Donora Valley in Pennsylvania in 1948, and in the Meuse Valley in Belgium in 1930. The "killer" smogs of London in 1952 resulted in more than 4,000 "excess" deaths. These kinds of data provide useful information for setting safe pollutant levels in the air.

The United States has developed national ambient standards based on such data, and the World Health Organization has similarly established guidelines that are employed in many countries throughout the world for similar purposes. But these health-based goals rely upon a model that assumes a relationship between concentration and impacts that is outlined in Figure 5.2a. As the concentration decreases, so do the impacts, and below a certain threshold, there is no effect. The U.S. standards also call for a "margin of safety," requiring that the ambient standard be set well below the threshold. But what if the real world looks like Figure 5.2b instead of Figure 5.2a? What if there is no threshold?

In such a case, there is no "margin of safety." In fact, there can be no "safe" level at all, since every level of pollutant could theoretically cause some damage. It might still be possible to employ the absolute control measure discussed earlier—prohibition—to protect us from the danger, but this may not always be an option (for example, some pollutants associated with combustion exhibit such a nonthreshold effect, but it is unlikely that we could prohibit all cases of combustion).

Figure 5.2b represents a case of environmental risk, rather than a safe, threshold condition, and scientists and regulatory officials wrestled with this type of problem throughout the 1970s and early 1980s. In 1983, the National Academy of Sciences (NAS) issued a report that split the problem into two parts. It suggested that the first task was to establish the nature and magnitude of the risk itself, through a process that was called risk assessment. This would be an objective, analytical process, conducted by the scientists themselves. The second task, risk management, was far messier, since it included political, social, and economic components, and

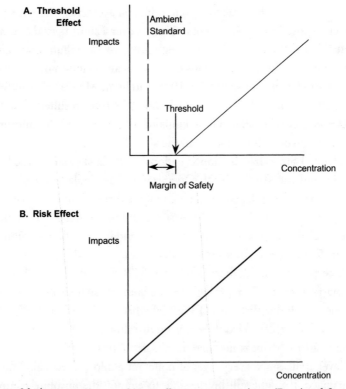

Figure 5.2.a,b. Response to ambient pollutant concentrations. (Reprinted from Roger Raufer, *Pollution Markets in a Green Country Town* with permission of Praeger Publishers, Westport, Connecticut, 1998.)

this was left to regulatory agencies such as the U.S. Environmental Protection Agency (EPA).

The risk assessment task had four steps: hazard identification, exposure assessment, dose response, and risk characterization. Cities now routinely perform risk assessments for infrastructure developments like trash incinerators or power plants. We conducted one such risk assessment here in Philadelphia for a trash burning facility to be built near the navy yard. This plant was very carefully designed with stringent pollution control systems, but no facility can remove 100 percent of the emissions. The Philadelphia risk assessment addressed fifteen pollutants, over six pathways of exposure: inhalation, dust ingestion, fish ingestion, dermal absorption, vegetable consumption, and soil ingestion.

To give an example of the risk assessment process, people might be exposed to pollution that settled down on their gardens. The assessment estimated this risk from such factors as the cross-sectional area of the average tomato (to estimate how much pollutant might settle down upon it), an assumption about how many garden vegetables people ate (younger persons would consume more than the elderly), and a conservative assumption that people would not wash these vegetables before consumption. Similarly, the risk assessment took into account children putting their hands in their mouth (and thus ingesting soil), and fishermen along the Delaware and Schuylkill Rivers who would eat their catch (and thus consume fish that might bioaccumulate the pollutants).

The risk assessment concluded that the "most exposed individual" would suffer an increased cancer risk from the trash burning facility of 10^{-6}, or one in a million. What exactly does this mean? The scientists who conducted the risk assessment report compared it to the risk of smoking two cigarettes over a seventy-year lifetime. It was similarly compared to drinking about forty cans of diet soda, because of the risk of saccharine.

Comparing risks is a controversial aspect of the risk management task, used to bring the findings of risk assessment into context for making decisions. How does the risk of such a trash burning facility compare with other risks that citizens might face? If we consider risks in terms of mortality (the chance of dying in a single year, rather than the cancer morbidity discussed above), then perhaps the most risky occupation is that of a movie stuntperson—the chance of a job-related death within a single year is about 1 in 100. That is, of 100 performers doing stunts, it is likely that

1 is going to die in a given year. As one goes down the list of occupations, the odds for race car drivers are about 10^{-3}, or 1 in 1000; then come firemen, farmers, miners, and police officers, at about 10^{-4}. Engineers, insurance agents, and city planning professors are much lower, at 10^{-5} or so, as these are not particularly hazardous occupations.

What about the risks from lifestyle? Smoking cigarettes is probably the most risky thing that many people do—the risks of smoking a pack a day are about 10^{-3}, up there with being a race car driver or engaging in sky diving or rock climbing. Your chances of death in an accident while canoeing, skiing, or fishing are about 10^{-5}.

Environmental risks from power plants and incinerators today are usually well below that, typically in the 10^{-6} range or below. These are similar to other environmental risks, such as the chance of dying from hurricanes, tornadoes, lightning, or animal bites. From the regulators' perspective, risks that are in the 10^{-6} range or below tend to be considered de minimis, and these are usually ignored. Risks that are 10^{-4} or above are usually considered significant, and tend to be addressed. But what about those in the range between 10^{-6} and 10^{-4}? The problem for regulators is that this is exactly the range where we tend to live our everyday lives. The result is that some problems are addressed in this range, and others are ignored; it depends upon the nature of the risk, the public's concern, and various other political, social, and economic factors.

In Philadelphia, the results of the risk assessment showed that the impacts of the proposed trash burning facility would be de minimis. But neighbors were not impressed and still considered it too risky, so the facility was never built. The public's view of environmental risk can differ considerably from that of experts, and, despite the seemingly "hard" numbers above, even experts have a very difficult time estimating the magnitude of environmental risks accurately. However, we are beginning to recognize that the world is more readily represented by the risk model than by the threshold model. Recently, the EPA decided to revise the environmental goals (i.e., the national ambient standards) for respirable particulate and ozone, and the science made clear that the risk model was more appropriate for these pollutants, even though the law still required an adequate margin of safety.

Today, scientists are trying to push beyond health risk assessments such as that described for Philadelphia's proposed trash plant, to address ecological and other environmental risks such as global warming or species extinction. In many cases, they are trying to stretch the NAS four-step process, adding additional components such as endpoint identification (are cancer and death the only appropriate indicators?) and feedback systems (i.e., "risk cascades") between the steps. The ultimate success of these new techniques for environmental goal setting has yet to be determined. But risk remains an important new element of environmental management and will help us to better define the environmental goals we have yet to achieve.

The Regulatory Means

The environmental regulatory approach outlined in Figure 5.1 was adopted in the United States and other countries, but it is not the only approach governments might adopt. Economists in particular have offered some perceptive criticism, suggesting that there might be a more inexpensive way to obtain comparable levels of environmental quality.

The alternative approach offered by economists is shown in Figure 5.3.

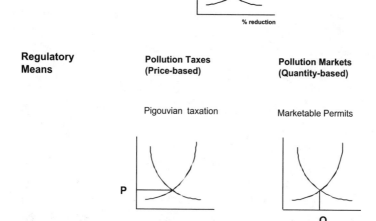

Figure 5.3. Economic regulatory approaches. (Roger Raufer)

In this case, the marginal costs of pollution control are compared with its marginal benefits. All of the information that went into setting the environmental quality standards—concerns about people's health, damage to forests and crops, and so forth—would be incorporated into the marginal benefit curve. Then, setting the proper environmental goal becomes obvious—it occurs at the point where marginal costs equal marginal benefits. If pollution control occurs beyond this point, then every additional dollar spent on control results in less than one dollar of environmental benefits. If the control falls below this point, then every additional dollar spent results in more than one dollar of environmental benefits, indicating that more should be done.

Much of the research in environmental economics over the past four decades has focused on how these marginal cost and benefit curves can be determined. But economists offer more than just this goal-setting approach; they also have some ideas about the means to achieve it. For, unfortunately, these curves are not like supply and demand curves—there is no invisible hand of the marketplace to take us there.

Economists offer two approaches to get us to the point where marginal costs equal marginal benefits. The first one, proposed in the 1920s by Cambridge professor Arthur Pigou, suggests that we tackle the problem from the price side and set a tax on the pollution. An alternative approach, proposed in 1968 by Professor John Dales of the University of Toronto, approaches it from the quantity side. This results in a market in "emission allowances," and just such an approach was employed in 1990 in the United States to control acid rain. The economists thus offer an alternative way to set environmental goals, and two alternative means to accomplish these goals, as shown in Figure 5.3.

Such economic mechanisms are not easy to implement, but they are helped by one important fact: After years of implementing command/control regulation, urban areas in the United States and other developed economies have begun to climb the marginal cost curve. It is thus becoming increasingly expensive to capture further emissions reductions. The past thirty-five years of environmental management might best be summarized by the observations noted in Box 5.1. It is particularly important to note that we now use a hybrid approach. We really don't have much faith yet in the economists' idea of using economics to set environmental goals, and prefer to stick with the surety of the science and public health ideas we

---

Box 5.1. Thirty-five Years of Experience in Environmental Management

- Command/control regulation won the early battles.
- Economics became increasingly important as society climbed the marginal cost curve.
- A hybrid regulatory system has been developed.
- This system keeps environmental goals set under the command/control approach, but employs economic regulatory means.
- The United States tends to prefer quantity-based economic mechanisms.
- European and other countries tend to prefer price-based mechanisms.
- The transition to economic mechanisms has been gradual, with incremental improvements to increase economic efficiency.
- There is increased reliance on advanced technological systems to measure emissions.
- The economic mechanisms rely on a regulatory infrastructure established under the command/control framework.

---

have traditionally employed to set environmental goals under command/control regulation. But we really do appreciate the tools that the economists offer to *achieve* environmental goals, and want to employ them to meet important command/control objectives. Thus a major transition is currently under way in urban areas of the United States: a shift from technology-oriented, command/control regulatory means to one that relies on economic incentives.

In the United States, we tend to prefer the quantity-based approach and have now developed markets for ozone control as well as acid rain. European countries and those in many other parts of the world tend to prefer the idea of price-based regulation, however, and thus employ pollution taxes and levies instead. It is interesting (and encouraging) to note that the whole debate about greenhouse gas control has been framed within this economic context. "Emissions trading" is a quantity-based approach to pollution control.

The Future of Urban Pollution Control

What happens when the new risk model meets the economic model in urban areas? One simple example is to rank the cost effectiveness of various new regulations in reducing premature deaths. Such analyses have been done, and one of the things they tend to show is that environmental regulations are not a particularly good means for reducing the public's health risks. Much of this is because we have already achieved the major public health advances associated with clean drinking water, solid waste management, and so forth, and new regulations simply don't achieve much improvement. The money is much better spent on medical interventions (i.e., drug treatment centers, immunizations for children, etc.); even consumer product safety regulation is far more cost effective.

Yet it is clear that we have major environmental issues that still need to be addressed. Global warming could be a major environmental ecosystem problem, even if it is not an immediate health problem. Some researchers suggest that higher levels of malaria and other diseases will accompany a shift of the breeding areas of vectors, but the health damages are likely to be secondary to other ecological changes. Similarly, ozone depletion, species extinction, and various other environmental problems need to be addressed—but public health issues are only one aspect of the reason for concern.

Individual cities will not solve these problems, but it is also clear that they must become part of the solution. Pollution control in the urban environment must therefore be framed by four considerations:

Many serious environmental issues now require a broader regulatory response (i.e., at the regional, national, or international level) than available at a municipal level, and cities will therefore have to subordinate their control programs accordingly.

Public health has traditionally been the major reason for urban pollution control, but it is time to move beyond that idea and focus on a more comprehensive view of the environment (to include local ecosystem damage, etc.).

Urban environmental management is still appropriate for local public health concerns, but such an approach must consider environmental risks.

Economic tools are becoming increasingly useful for accomplishing urban environmental goals.

Within the framework already established by national legislation, U.S. cities should have more discretion in making local decisions about pollution control improvements, particularly because the federal government has been reducing the amount of implementation money available to cities and states. Municipal governments have been hit with a series of "unfunded mandates" in the environmental arena, and while federal legislation is designed to limit that problem in the future, it does not address past requirements. In many cities, the marginal cost of such improvements is still very high for the level of risk reduction provided. Now that cities are operating in a "residual risk" environment (i.e., the risks that remain after initial efforts at pollution control have been accomplished), and now that they must provide most of the financing for implementing changes, they will demand a greater say in how that pollution control money is spent.

NOTES

1. T.M. Schmitz, "Pollution, Law, Science and Damage Awards," *Cleveland State Law Review,* 18 (September 1969).

2. P. Brimblecombe, "Attitudes and Responses Towards Air Pollution in Medieval England," *Journal of the Air Pollution Control Association,*vol. 26, no. 10 (October 1976).

3. Roger K. Raufer, *Pollution Markets in a Green Country Town: Urban Environmental Management in Transition,* (Westport, Conn.: Praeger, 1998).

C h a p t e r   6

Highway Planning and Land Use: Theory and Practice

Stephen H. Putman

The Invention of Premature Obsolescence

From the 1940s through the 1960s there were hundreds of "before-and-after studies" of highway bypasses that had been built around the centers of American cities and towns. Along with the federal funds to help pay for bypass construction came the obligation to examine what the consequences were. Some studies concluded that their bypass helped local commerce, others concluded that a bypass hurt local commerce. Although the results differed, the information in the studies was probably pretty accurate. Most of the studies were done after a bypass was completed, so it wasn't a matter of hypothesizing what would happen; it was a matter of observing what did happen. There is no evidence that anyone who prepared one of these studies ever seriously considered the implications of any of the others, or that the studies individually, or taken together, had any significant influence on highway policy. The difficulty lay in the fact that there was no formal structure within which to understand what was going on. Each study was an ad hoc investigation made in the absence of a comprehensive theory that could account for the relationships between transportation and land use. Further, there was no mechanism in place whereby the conclusions of the studies could be used to inform subsequent policy development or implementation.

One example of this gap between theory and practice is seen in the fact that often a piece of roadway which was meant to serve the public with efficient traffic flow for twenty-five years or more would become congested immediately upon its completion. This phenomenon was given a scientific-sounding name: the premature obsolescence of highway facilities.

Eventually the federal government decided it had better commission some research to discover the cause of this phenomenon. This led, in 1971, to the first research project that I did at the University of Pennsylvania, examining the relationships between transportation and land use. What I found by this research, which confirmed what many sensible people already knew, was that transportation influenced land use both by allowing, or facilitating, and by inducing, land development. This development, and there is still dispute in the field as to whether in any given region it is new development or relocated development, then created an immediate, unpredicted demand for use of the transportation facilities. What I did in that first research project was to formalize, in terms of a reasonably explicit structure that demonstrated the way in which transportation and land use were related to each other, what was known about transportation and land use interactions. At the same time, somewhat to the discomfort of the federal sponsors, I documented that, for the most part, throughout the United States, transportation and land use planning were being done by planning agencies in such a way as to guarantee that their forecasts, or estimates, or their impact studies generally, would yield incorrect results. This was because no agency was, at that time, making any attempt to directly link its transportation forecasts with its land use forecasts. It is unfortunate, but true, that in transportation planning not much has changed since then.

I went on to spend what is now almost thirty years trying to convince people in the transportation planning profession that they really ought to change, most particularly by the use of better land use forecast inputs, the way in which they do highway planning; that, in other words, they should try to do a better job of anticipating the consequences of their actions.

Historical and Political Context

Radial highways, that is, highways radiating out from metropolitan centers, were still being built in the early 1970s. The notion was that these highways would allow some portion of the populace to live in the suburbs, where they said they wished to live, free from traffic congestion and other unpleasant consequences of urban crowding, and commute into the cities to work. While this was, in many cases the short-term effect, the long-term results have proven to be strikingly different from what was anticipated. Employment moved out to where the people were living. As a result, the expected beneficial consequences of these highway projects were submerged in a tidal wave of rearrangements of metropolitan spatial patterns. Today, we have the entirely unexpected phenomenon of circumferential commuting being, in some regions, the dominant feature of regional commuting patterns. The employment and residence location patterns attendant upon this phenomenon are also entirely contrary to what was initially expected.

For some reason this spectacular failure of highway planning coincided with a loss of interest in federal funding for transportation research not directly associated with the mechanics of transportation. Thus not much was done about transportation and land use interrelationships until the late 1980s when, with people becoming increasingly concerned with air quality issues, planners' attention turned to the relationships between transportation, land use, and air quality.

The 1991 amendments to the Clean Air Act, and the Intermodal Surface Transportation Efficiency Act (ISTEA) had a significant, though perhaps transient, effect on transportation and land use planning and research. The two acts taken together required that for any metropolitan area with a population in excess of 250,000, if that area was in air quality nonattainment status (i.e., not meeting Clean Air Act standards), no federal money could be spent on transportation improvements unless it could be demonstrated that those transportation improvements would "not be harmful to" air quality. A later amendment changed that to read, will "improve" air quality.

California already had somewhat similar legislation. It required that any agency proposing to change the transportation system had to demonstrate that the change would improve air quality. Now, if you analyze any piece (link or set of links) of a highway network where there is heavy congestion, you find numerous vehicles moving slowly, stopping and starting, and thereby producing their maximum level of emissions. In such situations, if you simply construct an additional highway lane, then all the vehicles move more rapidly, and there are fewer stops and starts. Emissions go down. Based on this change, you can assert that the construction of the new lane has improved air quality. The problem is, if you then actually construct the new lane, and add lanes to other highways, the new capacity keeps inducing more traffic and more emissions. In effect, you subject more people to more emissions spread over a larger area. Thus you end up with the conditions that resulted in the framing of the two federal acts.

Sections of the Clean Air Act amendments (CAAA) and ISTEA were written, in part, to prevent precisely this sort of piecemeal application of their requirements. They required that the means by which the air quality consequences of the transportation system are calculated show a "consistency" (actually the language of an earlier version of the act used the term "equilibrium") between the transportation forecasts and the land use forecasts. This meant, in practice, that when one did the air quality calculation, it was to come at the end of a sequence of calculations that took into account transportation system changes and the land use consequences of those changes, forecast twenty, thirty, or forty years into the future, by use of an integrated transportation and land use analysis procedure that could correctly capture the interrelationships. The overall structure of these interactions is shown in Figure 6.1.

This was a very good idea. It also mandated a very difficult task that

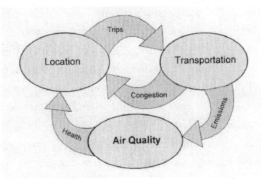

Figure 6.1. The interrelationships among transportation, land use, and air quality. (Steve Putman)

provided me with a lot of consulting work for a decade or more. It provided a number of students both the data and the topics for dissertations. In some places it may actually have affected public policy decisions about transportation construction. Unfortunately, despite the existence of this admirable legislation, only a small percentage of metropolitan planning organizations (MPOs) around the country adopted this approach to integrating transportation and land use forecasting. In the past five years or so, an increasing number of even this small band of pioneering MPOs have drifted back to their old ways because they have discovered that the federal government has not been enforcing the acts.

If the federal government were to enforce the law, there would undoubtedly be places where local governments would be required to place restrictions both on land development and on highway construction. That would probably be a very unpopular action. Local governments and local politicians would also be required to tell the public that, in many places, they were not going to be able to do much about traffic congestion. It is my guess that no one in political office wants to stand up and say that. The same is true for air quality. If the government were to actually enforce the Clean Air Act, there are places where the U.S. Environmental Protection Agency (EPA) would have to say, "You can't build because you are in nonattainment status. You can't build any more highways, ever." There would be a lot of political problems. I think that this is the principal reason why the acts are not being enforced with respect to transportation and land use planning.

ISTEA and the Clean Air Act amendments were, perhaps, too powerful a legislative tool, too "heavy a hammer." The consequences were too big a burden for the politicians to bear. Imagine if you, as a technical staff person, were to go in and tell them, the politicians, "Sorry, we didn't do the modeling right. We didn't use an integrated transportation and land use modeling procedure, and the Feds are holding back our transportation funds." Most politicians wouldn't have a clue as to what you were talking about. All they would know was that there were an awful lot of important people in their region who were going to be pretty miffed because all those millions of transportation dollars were being kept in Washington and not given to them to be spent in their region. Even so, in order to have a reasonable chance at producing reliable forecasts, both for transportation facilities and for land use, there must be a formal link between the analyses. It is not a matter of its being too difficult, technically, to make this connection. It is a matter of its being very difficult, or too difficult, politically, within the planning agencies.

The Linked Transportation and Land Use Planning Approach

In the mid-1990s, a lawsuit was brought under the National Environmental Policy Act (NEPA) by the Sierra Club, Illinois Chapter, and others, against the U.S. Department of Transportation, the Illinois Department of Transportation (IDOT) and the Illinois State Toll Highway Authority. This was because they made use of a set of forecasts to determine whether or not they should build a piece of interstate highway; and those forecasts had been prepared the "old" way, without reference to the new procedures required by ISTEA. The way in which transportation planning has traditionally been done, and the way it still is done by a substantial majority of transportation agencies, is that the agencies produce or obtain forecasts of where people are going to live and work throughout the region, out to some planning horizon, let us say the year 2030. This "land use" forecast then would be used as input for their transportation planning. Typically, these forecasts would have been produced by the "socioeconomic," or "land use" division of the planning agency, or in some cases the agency might arrange to get the forecast elsewhere, outside the agency. In this Illinois case, in Chicago, the transportation modeling is done by the Chicago Area Transportation Study (CATS), and the land use and socioeconomic work is done by the Northeastern Illinois Planning Commission (NIPC). NIPC produced the land use forecast, CATS produced the transportation forecast, each completely separately, in the same way as they had been doing for as long as anyone could remember. There was no investigation of the effects of the planned transportation improvements on land use at different stages of development. In the language of the court document, produced in 1997, "Plaintiffs point out, and defendants admit, that defendants used a single unvarying land use population and employment forecast for analyzing all alternatives, including the no action alternative."

This continues, despite the above and other lawsuits, to be absolutely standard procedure. I recently saw a survey of all twenty-five MPOs in the state of Florida. About ten or twelve are for regions in excess of 250,000 population. No MPOs in Florida do integrated transportation and land use forecasting. They all do them separately. They start with a land use forecast and then run the transportation models, which are extremely complicated, and they surround them with great walls of jargon. This has the effect of preventing most of the other, nontransportation, planning people from having any kind of intelligent interaction with transportation planners or plans. The transportation planners appear to like it that way. It's not that they are evil, it's just that they are clever about protecting their agency "turf," and their money. They do get the money. Spending on transportation research and transportation modeling is perhaps two orders of magnitude greater than spending on land use research and land use modeling, and has been that way for forty years. All the multibillion-dollar transportation projects will include millions of dollars of transportation modeling, but it would be very unusual if they spent $50,000 on the economic and land use forecast inputs to the transportation modeling. Yet, it is perfectly obvious that the results of the transportation modeling efforts are dependent upon the quality of their inputs.

In any case, using the socioeconomic and land use forecast inputs, the transportation modeling process follows what is known as the "four-step process." The first step calculates the number of trips originating from and terminating in each of the sub-areas into which the region will have been divided for analysis purposes. These sub-areas are called traffic analysis zones. Once the trip generation calculations have been completed, then in the second step the trip distribution is calculated, estimating for each zone how many trips go to and come from each zone. Once this matrix of trips is estimated, in the third step the trips are split up by modes; single occupant vehicles (automobiles), multioccupant vehicles, light and/or heavy rail transit, and so forth. Then, in the fourth step, the agency runs the trip assignment procedures, which calculate, according to various criteria as may be specified by the software user, the routes that the trips, meaning the trip makers, will take through the network to get from each origin zone to each destination zone. In determining those routes they use a mathematical representation of the highway system, which will be described in terms of what are called links (pieces of the network) and nodes, the places where the pieces of networks connect. The assignment problem is to find out how, via what paths, the trips are likely to traverse the links. Finally, what we hope the agency does (some of them, even the very large ones, still do not even do this) is to calculate whether the trips traveling each link exceed a nominal link-specific capacity, expressed in terms of vehicles per hour, which is the maximum number of trips that can use the link before congestion results appear. At present, it is safe to assume that just about every MPO follows this method. The vast majority do it with one of four or five different proprietary software packages.

Note how this entire edifice of calculation is built on the initial socioeconomic and land use forecasts. There is, when using the "four-step process," no procedure for looking at the possibility of traffic that may be allowed, encouraged, or induced by the act of creating the highway, although the fact that this additional traffic is bound to appear is well known. The socioeconomic and land use forecasts themselves are almost always "end-state" forecasts for a time period, say, thirty years in the future, and such long-range forecasts are notoriously unreliable. Given that these socioeconomic and land use forecasts exist before the transportation modeling is done, there is no reason why planners couldn't do the year 2030 traffic analysis before the year 2020 traffic analysis. This should be a warning signal, because we are supposedly aware of the fact that, to the extent that we perceive it, time goes in one direction. If we don't know what the forecast for 2020 looks like, then it is not likely that we can do a good job of figuring out what 2030 is going to look like. But, in traditional transportation forecasting, there is no temporal dimension of the sort that would require year 2020 analyses to be done prior to year 2030 analyses.

When Are Forecasts Plans, or Plans Forecasts?

Transportation planners, generally, don't want to get involved in the messiness of land use forecasting, nor do they want to be involved in the even messier process of land use planning. There is quite a lot of confusion, especially among politicians and persons higher up in planning agencies, between "forecasting," a term we generally understand to mean using some method to make an estimate of a probable future and what I, and others, call "plancasting." Plancasting is a process whereby we impose our plans, our goals, our criteria for good or bad urban form, on the forecasting method and thus produce a "forecast" that represents more the way we would like the future to be, rather than what the statistical analyses which underpin the forecast method would calculate the future to be.

It is critically important to know that the socioeconomic and land use forecasts—whether they are accurate or not—become the basis for what is, de facto, a regional plan. These forecasts, as inputs to the four-step process for determining transportation needs and transportation projects, thus affect the planning and implementation of a region's transportation infrastructure. As both the existing and the proposed highways will ultimately have a strong influence on the land use patterns of the area, both the land use inputs and the travel forecast outputs are, albeit indirectly, significant determinants of a region's future. Sometimes the importance of these forecasts is understood, perhaps argued over, sometimes negotiated. More often they are wholly prepared, questions resolved, and results promulgated at a staff level by people who would be horrified to be told they are doing regional planning. In fact, they are making every effort to avoid doing so. It is, they might say, "not their job."

How is the land use forecast done? It is often done by extrapolation; by taking current growth rates and projecting them along a straight line into the future. Sometimes it is done by land use models of one sort or another, but typically the land-use planners and forecasters all follow the defective path of getting a set of travel times from the transportation models in advance of doing the land use forecasting. We know that if the trips assigned to the highway networks change, the congestion level will change. If the congestion levels change, the time and cost of travel will change. We also know that people make location decisions based, in part, on travel times and costs. Thus transportation affects land use patterns, and the trip volumes generated by these land use patterns affect network congestion. So, in the same way that the transportation planners are going to have a set of land use forecasts for their purposes which are fixed, or invariant, the land use planners, if they use transportation information at all, are going to get fixed forecasts of travel times and costs from the transportation people before they have designed and studied their transportation network.

Chicago, a large, cosmopolitan, and sophisticated metropolitan area, did all of its land use forecasting in the absence of any information about the transportation system, up until about five years ago. Now, they do something different, partly because, at least at NIPC, they anticipated the problems that would eventually come as a consequence of this myopic forecasting process, and they hired me to help them implement a set of models that would change their approach. They are not being sued for their current work; they are being sued for their past work.

The immediate cause of the Chicago lawsuit was that CATS, the transportation planning agency for the region, in conjunction with IDOT, was required to do an evaluation of the consequences of building a major new piece of highway in the southern part of the Chicago area. CATS proceeded to ask NIPC for land use forecasts, which were provided. CATS used those forecasts to estimate the traffic in the area, then CATS changed the transportation network to include some lane widenings, as well as the new highway they were going to build. Then, using the same set of NIPC land use forecasts, they calculated what the new congestion levels would be and were able to demonstrate that, once they improved the transportation system, they would reduce the levels of congestion and everything would be wonderful. They are in court because they used a set of constant land use inputs for all the different policy evaluations. They had produced multiple sets of forecasts for the years 2000, 2010, and 2020. The problem was that their transportation forecasts of the consequences of building the new highway made use of the same land-use forecast inputs (for all time points) as did the transportation forecasts of the consequences of *not building* the new highway. In this way they completely excluded the possibility of any change in land use as a consequence of the proposed highway construction. Opponents of the construction of the facilities, principally because of the potential of these facilities to exacerbate already existing land use sprawl in the region, took the opportunity to bring suit. Increasingly, individuals and groups concerned with the environmental and sustainability consequences of regional sprawl are becoming more sophisticated in their understanding of the technical processes that underlie transportation and land use forecasting and policy analysis. They can take aim at the weak points in the process in an attempt to challenge and subsequently change the way regional planning is done.

In some places, forecasting is understood as a very significant component of regional planning. The members of the technical staff at the regional planning agency understand that the forecasts have both direct and indirect effects on any decision, and therefore they involve the local planning community in the preparation of the forecasts. They include not just official planners, but real estate professionals and developers, utility companies, and others who are interested in the way in which the region is evolving. In places where they do this well, such as Phoenix or Dallas–Fort Worth, they have what they call technical advisory committees to the planning agency. When the agency staff starts a new round of regional forecasts, it uses a computer modeling procedure to make a forecast five years into the future. They then review the forecast with their technical advisory committee. Further, they have a procedural mechanism for going back and forth between the computer model and the committee until there is an agreement on the first five-year forecast. They then make the next, subsequent, five-year forecast and do the same thing. By this means both the transportation and the land use computer modeling become part of a consistent procedure that augments the statistical results with input from people who are familiar with what is going on in the region.

Even in this situation, however, the forecast is not really understood as being, de facto, a plan. Yet, in many regions, because of the effect of transportation on land use, the forecasts produced as a part of regional transportation planning are often the closest thing to a regional plan for the area that ever gets produced.

If you really go to the root of this, in order to develop policies that have any hope of guiding a region toward the goals of its regional plan, the analysis of policy must be done with methods that embody a linked view of transportation and land use phenomena. Further, in order to have any hope of implementing such policies as are developed, you need a regional government or a regional planning authority with the tools to control and/or enforce policies, of which transportation is only one component. This authority would have to be capable of saying, "We are just not going to put any more sewers in there. We are just not going to build any more highways out there. We are just not going to give any more building permits, and so forth." That would be a necessary concomitant of real regional planning.

Something that bears watching is happening in Atlanta, Georgia, an area that has been seriously out of compliance with federal clean air standards for many years. The EPA had set mid-January 1998 as a deadline for completing a compliance plan, but was prepared to "grandfather" a whole series of projects so that highway building could go on as usual after the deadline. However, citizens' groups filed a lawsuit in federal court challenging the way that these projects were going to be permitted to go forward. Faced with this court challenge, the state agreed to a settlement that put most of these projects on hold. Now the state has created a Georgia Regional Transportation Authority and is committed to putting together a comprehensive transportation plan that will include rapid transit and new kinds of land use planning so the Atlanta region can meet federal air quality standards. If the Authority succeeds, it will become much more likely that the law will be enforced in other metropolitan areas with serious non-compliance problems.

What Can Be Done to Change the Situation?

What many planners were hoping from the Clean Air Act and ISTEA was that, in addition to addressing air quality, they would be able to use air quality as a lever to get at another whole class of problems, the sprawl and sprawl-related problems. It is my guess that, if we are going to meet the explicit air quality goals of this legislation, we will do it with technology, by building vehicles that emit very low levels of pollution. The prototypes for such vehicles already exist; it is just a matter of time and political pressure until they are on the road in significant numbers. Yet this will not resolve the greater issue, the one of metropolitan sprawl and sustainability.

I have a favorite description of the extreme case, which illustrates the point. Suppose that in tomorrow's newspaper we read of an amazing new technological breakthrough. For a nominal price, people could have a gray plastic disk installed outside their house. It would be about 3 or 4 feet in diameter and mounted on a small raised platform. A person could stand on this disk, carrying a small amount of stuff, say a briefcase or a bag of tools, and then punch in a set of coordinates using a handheld device like a television remote control unit (given the problems many people have with their VCR controllers, these units could also be purchased prepro-grammed). After a few seconds' time, the person would simply vanish, and shortly thereafter, would appear on a similar disk at the destination identified by the coordinates. The device would use considerable energy, but the energy would be produced regionally and then be distributed by the utility company, and would thus have minimal environmental impact. The components of the disk could be made of recycled fast-food containers. With this device, the air-quality consequences of home-to-work commuting would be eliminated. Would regional planners be pleased with this technology? Think of the consequences for employment and residence location. You could live almost anywhere and work almost anywhere. While the air quality issue might thus be resolved, the sprawl problem would be extreme.

Unfortunately, the current air quality and transportation legislation does not directly deal with the issues of sprawl and sustainability. These issues, however, will be a major challenge to planners and policymakers in the years ahead.

Recommendations

1. Amend and enforce federal transportation legislation.
A rather simple change, with complex and probably mostly beneficial consequences, would be to make the language of the act clearly state that all transportation forecasts and all land use forecasts must meet a minimum of two requirements. First, the one cannot ever be done without direct and explicit links to the other. Second no forecasting approach should be permitted where it is possible to produce the year 2030 forecast before producing the year 2020 forecast. More difficult, but essential, would be a move on the part of the appropriate agencies to enforce the legislation

2. Create joint regional transportation and land use planning authorities.
If any of the major regional problems are to be successfully addressed, regional planning will have to deal directly with sprawl and sustainability. Perhaps METRO in Portland, Oregon, or the new Georgia Regional Transportation Authority in Atlanta, if it succeeds, could be the models. Regional policy issues now hidden in the land use and transportation forecasts should be brought into the open, discussed, and decided in a public process by these regional agencies.

PART 3

Education, Safety, and Welfare

C h a p t e r   7

Improving Primary and Secondary Education

Susan H. Fuhrman

People at both state and national levels identify education as the most important policy issue on America's agenda. Education has been considered one of the three key policy issues for the past fifteen years, maybe almost twenty years, and each year its importance seems to increase.

First of all, we are moving toward a "knowledge society," Peter Drucker's term. If we want a productive and successful economy in the future, we have to depend much more on knowledge and skills than in the past, when we were a manufacturing society.

Second, while the economy is booming now, it is increasingly becoming a winner-take-all economy. Gaps between the lower income groups and the affluent are growing at the same time that the economy is booming. Historically, education has served as a leveler, a route to upward mobility for those who need it.

Also helping to boost education's place on the public agenda is the increasing diversity of American society, the increasing number of immigrants. Again, education has historically played a role in assimilation and acculturation. It is an important route to producing one society.

In case we need another reason to keep education at the top of our national agenda, we seem to be fixing other problems. Welfare appears to have been reformed—not true, but some people think so. Crime is down, drug and alcohol abuse, teenage pregnancy, all these statistics are going down while education remains a problem.

By all the major measures, and in all the major subjects, educational achievement has been virtually stagnant for the past twenty years. There were some gains in the 1970s, but they were wiped out in the later seventies and the eighties; then there was some recovery in the nineties, which all results in no overall change. The fact that educational achievement has been static for twenty years may be more favorable than it looks, as, in the interim, our society has become poorer and more diverse, there are more single parents, and so on. But, in any case, education is not keeping up with what people foresee as the needs of the next century's workforce.

Also, we are not keeping up internationally. We recently received results from the *Third International Math and Science Study*. Americans are at the top of the world in the fourth grade—number two in math and number seven in science. They reach the middle by the eighth grade and are at the bottom by the twelfth grade. We are the only country that does not maintain its previous position over those years.

Why? Everything we know about these international results so far is at the country level; student-level data have not been analyzed yet, but we have a good idea what is going on.

Problems in U.S. Education

In the United States we have fifteen thousand local districts deciding their own curricula; they choose which topics they are going to cover. The result is a very decentralized, fragmented education system. Our national textbook publishers try to sell to as broad a market as possible. They cover every topic superficially. So, for example, our texts in eighth grade math have thirty-five topics, and the corresponding Japanese textbook has nine. There is a lack of focus and a lack of depth in our curriculum; this has to be a major reason for our comparatively poor performance. Another problem: we aim low. In the math curriculum we actually do fine up to the fourth grade, and then we start repeating what we taught from kindergarten through grade three.

We also don't have the respect for education, for the teachers, for the classroom that other countries have. A comparative study that videotaped classrooms in Germany, Japan, and the United States found that in American classrooms instruction was interrupted 31 percent of the time. In Germany 15 percent, in Japan never. The classroom in Japan is sacrosanct, teaching is in progress. American classrooms get interrupted for anything. The public address system announces the bus schedules. People don't really focus on it, but how much instruction can possibly go on in such a teaching environment?

So achievement has been relatively stagnant. There was some improvement in the seventies, probably due to a rise in the parental education level. But then it declined again, and, despite some recent improvement, achievement levels remain a major concern. The gap in income levels is certainly based on educational achievement, and the gap is persistent and big.

Teacher quality is another big issue, particularly in urban areas: 25 percent of teachers nationally are not qualified to teach the subjects they are assigned; they have no appropriate credentials, and the assignment can only be justified on an emergency basis. In some fields, the situation is even worse. About half of the math and science teachers are teaching out of their field. And it is worse in urban areas than in suburban areas. The youngest, least experienced teachers are assigned to the most troubled schools, and the more senior teachers with some experience get to choose, which usually means they opt for an easier post. This occurs often in large cities. Schools with poor kids who need extra help are the ones that are assigned people who are unqualified in the subjects they are teaching, based on some kind of temporary, emergency justification.

Another major issue is bureaucratization, and the interaction of bureaucracy with the unions. We have bureaucratic regulation in part because we have relied on process requirements to insure some standards despite decentralization of authority. We need to have some level of equal treatment across schools. How else but by states requiring that everybody offers science? How else but by districts requiring that every schoolchild is taught math for forty-five minutes each day? It is very difficult to make changes in these systems. These regulations prove persistent and they tend to be largely about process and not content. Other countries don't have the same problem. They have a national curriculum. They say, we don't care how long you teach this topic, you teach it, that's all.

A national curriculum gives other countries another advantage. Their teachers are prepared for it. Our teacher training often does not relate to the curriculum because there is no common agreed upon curriculum. In other countries, professional development, continuing education for teachers, focuses on a curriculum that everybody knows. In our country, it is whatever schools choose. A school might have a workshop on the right brain, or the left brain, or sometimes both, but they do not have a consistent professional development program that relates to the curriculum.

Another problem: Our infrastructure is old; school buildings are decaying, particularly in the cities. Many schools were built a hundred years ago, at the time of the great expansion in public education related to peak years of immigration. Another expansion took place during the building boom in the post–World War II period, the baby boomers' schools. Those schools are now fifty years old. In many cases this aging physical plant has not been maintained well. Deteriorating buildings, with systems that don't function, make all our other education problems worse.

Schools are embedded in the society in which they exist, when there are schools in high crime, high poverty areas these problems come into the schools. There is a need to keep order and to protect the students and teachers, to keep weapons out of the building, for example. Schools are asked to take on community services, to have medical and other health care services in their buildings, to reach out to the community. Schools become responsible for a lot of other tasks besides teaching and learning as the number of single parents grows and we get a more diverse and in some cases poorer population.

So there are lots of issues to worry about in education. Fortunately there are many people who want to do something about these problems. Let us look at a range of solutions.

A Consensus for Curriculum Standards

We have come to an agreement nationally that we have to somehow remedy the extreme decentralization of our curriculum and decide what should be taught. We have a consensus that we should reset our standards, our expectations, for learning, and they should apply to our whole society. What people have come to agree on is that the states should take the lead. In each subject area, states are setting standards for learning.

The standards are widely discrepant from state to state in format and specificity and in the ways to guide instruction, although all the states are working from national models of content. For example, each state is setting its math standards based on what the National Council of Teachers of

Mathematics says we should be trying to achieve; but how much they say a student should learn at each grade level, how detailed they get about the different content areas, how many examples they give, all vary from state to state. There have been three different efforts to rate or evaluate state standards by independent groups, and these scores are also very discrepant. There is very little overlap in the ways these national groups rate the states.

But at least the conversation has changed. People say we should agree about what students should learn. This is still different from countries where there is a very specific national curriculum. But it is a step in that direction. The idea behind these standards is that we will see more coordination than we used to. When schools develop specific curriculums, they will be tied to achieving the standards. When textbook publishers develop textbooks, they will be designed with the standards in mind. When teacher-education programs are carried out, they will be tied to the curriculum, so teachers will know what the students are expected to know. When professional development is designed, it will be tied to the standards. Teachers will improve their credentials in areas linked to the student curriculum. Perhaps, most critically, when we test students' knowledge, we can test based on what they are expected to know; which, believe it or not, we have not been able to do up to now.

All these years evaluation tests were designed by private testing companies to be curriculum-free because they wanted to compare students in differing curriculums across the country. So they were actually testing aptitude rather than achievement. We have never had good measures of what students were learning, because we never had a curriculum-based assessment. Now, states are trying to link their assessments to these standards and measure how well students are actually learning.

There is currently a major debate concerning whether we should also have a national test linked to standards. President Clinton once proposed a national standard, but he has not given the idea much visibility since the Contract with America. When the Republicans took over the Congress in early 1995 the idea of having a national test foundered, as Republicans traditionally get very nervous at the thought of anything that might lead to more federal control.

A national test based on standards would allow us to compare students across the country on specific content areas, something we can't do now. We do have a national test, the National Assessment for Educational

Progress, but it is based on samples; not every student is being tested. We don't have data on individual students, schools, or districts below the state level. A national test linked to standards could provide us with much more information, and it would have meaning for individual students; they could find out how they did.

Three Areas of Debate

There is now general agreement among states, school districts, and even publishers and private testing agencies that there should be curriculum standards. But, on the other reform issues, there is a lot of debate within this overall agreement about standards. There are three major areas of disagreement in areas of accountability, governance, and capacity.

Accountability

One big debate is over accountability. We are developing tests that are aligned to standards within states; that is, these are state standards that already exist, not the national standards that are still being debated. Schools would be held accountable for progress on these tests, and students would have to make progress over time. If they didn't make progress, the state would intervene. This could also be feasible at the city and district levels.

The district would hold individual schools accountable, which is what happened in Philadelphia. There is an index, and if the schools don't do well, they are seen as in decline, needing help. They get extra assistance, although there isn't always enough funding to give all the assistance that is really needed. School performance is expected to turn around. If it doesn't improve, ultimately, in thirty-three states the state would have authority to close schools that are doing badly. Students are allowed to go to other schools, or the schools are reopened with new staff. There is a range of remedies. On the other side, these new accountability systems also include rewards for the schools that are doing well.

There are a lot of people who believe that this kind of accountability is absolutely the key to improvement. If a firm does not do well, it does not sell its goods; it goes out of business. If it does well, there is a profit, the shareholders are happy. That is accountability. People have been saying that in education we haven't had accountability because, in the past, if test scores didn't go up, nothing happened. If test scores went down, nothing happened. Schools just stayed the same. I am sure there were interventions by individuals, superintendents of school districts or principals. But by nature these interventions were scattered, and sometimes they happened and sometimes they did not.

Part of the problem was that the unions were seen as very protective of people's jobs. Also the remedies available to the state had been limited. Theoretically, if a school district didn't do well, the state could cut off its aid, but this would produce a real predicament: You couldn't take away the aid because that would harm the children and not those responsible for poor achievement.

However, accountability is a big issue right now. We are talking about holding the schools accountable, giving schools reward money if they do better, closing them down if they do badly; increasingly school systems are holding principals accountable: They will lose their jobs if schools are not doing well. We are also talking about holding teachers accountable in places where schools are being closed. President Clinton wants to encourage the states to be even stronger on accountability. He is saying that federal money should not be given to states unless they have a strong accountability system, unless they close failing schools.

Another part of this thrust is to make students more accountable. In other countries, promotion is much more dependent on student achievement. In our country, we have gone back and forth historically between just promoting students no matter how poorly they do and holding them back and making them repeat a year if they don't do well. What is happening right now is people, including President Clinton, are saying that we should not be promoting students if they do not do well. No more social promotion, which is promotion with the age-cohort.

Unfortunately, the research shows that if you hold students back a year, they don't learn any more and they are many more times likely to drop out because their age makes them socially uncomfortable. So we are learning that we need to provide a lot of extra help for students who might not do well, so that they can be promoted. The president is proposing extra money in his budget. Some of it will go to help schools with lots of students at risk, allowing them to have extended days or Saturday classes or other programs they might need. But still people worry that there won't be enough money. Just doing away with social promotion without providing the necessary support for the students means we'll just have a lot of students failing and repeating, failing and dropping out. A student who drops out of the school system has a very limited future in an information-based society, so that dropping out of school is a much less acceptable outcome than it may have been in the past.

However, on the subject of accountability programs in general, some of the states have been doing this for a while and research shows that giving bonuses or threatening sanctions does cause people to focus attention on results. Teachers value the bonuses, not as strongly as they value students' learning, but it is among the things they feel are valuable. They fear the sanctions, so they are keyed up. But it is only a part of the solution. By itself, accountability is not going to improve instruction.

Governance

Another whole reform approach is to change the governance system. There are many people in this country who believe that the answer is to get rid of bureaucratization and unionization—give schools as much flexibility as possible and give parents a lot of flexibility about which schools to choose. So there are movements to use vouchers to give parents the money to choose either public or private schools and to start schools that are outside the system called charter schools. These schools are not part of the school district but are run by small groups of parents or teachers who want to follow a particular education approach, and, again, students could choose to go to them. If students left the Philadelphia school district to go to a charter, the money that Philadelphia would receive from the state would flow to the charter school. In many states, the entire per pupil allowance that the district would have spent on a child in a public school would follow the child to the charter. State and local money would go to the charter, and the public school district would lose the money. The theory is the district would try to compete by improving its own schools and getting the students back. That is the basic theory underlying these programs of choice, whether it involves private schools or not. There will be competition, and competition will, by its nature, improve schools.

Over thirty-five states have charter legislation. There are almost two thousand charter schools by now. There are a number of cities that have voucher programs. In Milwaukee and Ohio vouchers are publicly funded. In Indianapolis there is a privately funded one. In Texas there is the Edgewater school district, where everybody in the school district has a right to a voucher with private funding. There are many cities, Washington, D.C., and others, where there are privately donated scholarship funds for low-income children.

Governor Ridge of Pennsylvania is also proposing a voucher for low-income children, which would mean that the family will get the money and the kids could take that money to any school they choose, public or private.

There are a lot of issues involved here. First of all, it is not clear whether it is constitutional to take public money to a parochial school or a religious school. For many years, such actions would have been seen as abridging the First Amendment's separation of church and state. Even if the government were to inspect these schools to make sure the money was going to secular purposes, it would still be seen as too much entanglement between church and state. However, a Wisconsin court said that by forbidding public money to go to parochial schools, the government is in fact discriminating against religion, which is also forbidden by the First Amendment. Many people think the U.S. Supreme Court will go the same way when the issue reaches it. In some states where the state constitution exclusively forbids state aid to religious institutions, such aid may still be unconstitutional. This issue is going to be fought out in the courts over the next several years.

Assuming it is constitutional to include religious schools, there are still real questions of ideology and practicality about the voucher system. There are people who worry about further fragmentation of society if people go off into the private schools and don't stay with the public school system, which was always seen as the great socializer. There are concerns that, even if everybody were given a voucher, there are only a limited number of private schools. If vouchers go to everybody, it would be a windfall to the parents who already have children in private schools; they would get tax money back that they had resigned themselves to never seeing. But could private schools ever accommodate more than 10 to 15 percent of the children in a region?

If not, and we are paying all of our attention to vouchers as the solution, what about the 85 percent who are left behind? What kind of leverage does such a limited amount of competition actually provide for improving the system?

If we limit vouchers to low income people because they are the ones we really want to help, there are certain parents who are actively involved in their kid's education and who are the ones who will make use of the vouchers. But there are also parents who are less interested who will not follow up on the vouchers. There is a real potential for voucher systems to further stratify society.

Another question: The money being given out in a voucher system often does not cover the tuition in any school that we know of. The $700 voucher Governor Ridge is talking about is really symbolic; low-income families will still have to pay the rest of the tuition or be given a scholarship.

Finally, the evidence on the effect of charters and choice is very mixed. The presumption that increasing competition leads to better educational quality has not been proven yet. There will be those who deduce, because we haven't really done research on this, that children in private schools sometimes do better than their public school counterparts; but we have no evidence that better performance by students in private schools has ever had the effect of improving the instruction in public schools so they could get the students back.

Capacity

Nothing I have said about accountability or governance has much to do with the quality of the teaching force, but this is the major, basic, underlying issue. We can have all the charters we want but that doesn't mean we are going to have qualified teachers. So another way to attack educational problems would be to work on capacity, improving the skills of teachers. This could be accomplished in a whole range of ways, starting with higher standards for teacher education, higher salaries along with higher standards to attract teachers, better pay scales, and promoting people based on better criteria than we now use.

General salary levels for teachers were established at a time when teaching was seen as largely for women, who didn't have many other career options. So there is trouble in competing now that men and women have equal opportunities. Teaching salaries are not only low paying but are also flat; teachers can go in for a decent beginning salary, but long-term the salary doesn't increase by much. It generally tops out at about $60,000. This is not characteristic of careers that require so much education.

Typically teaching salaries go up with seniority, and then if a teacher takes a certain number of credits, he or she will get extra salary above that.

But the credits could be in anything. They would not necessarily have to be in the teacher's particular subject. A teacher could take underwater basket weaving and still get a raise. Frequently teachers take extra credits in administration; they all get certified to be principals. They don't become principals; they remain teachers and have not learned anything more about teaching from all those extra credits.

So, we are working on ways to reconstruct the salary scale more around knowledge and skills of teachers rather than around experience and credits. There is something called National Board Certification now, which is new in teaching. A teacher can apply to become certified nationally as an advanced teacher. It costs a lot of money, but about thirty states have said they will put up the money if the teachers want to do it. Getting this recognition should give teachers a substantial salary boost. The more credibility the National Board gets, the more districts should be willing to reward teachers who have gotten this advanced certification.

We also need to think about improving the capacity of students. There are a variety of interventions that do that. Most of them are preschool; we know that if we intervene early and the kids get rich experiences every day, they do better. Helpful interventions include more social services for kids who are hungry, and more work with parents so they can help kids. There are programs like family math and family literacy where everybody learns together.

We need to build the capacity of the system as well. We don't have a lot of good curriculum material that ties to these new standards. We need to get such materials developed. We need states and districts to hire people who can help schools. They don't have such people. President Clinton wants to ask states to turn around failing schools without knowing whether states know how to turn around failing schools. Most don't. So there are many things to do under the heading of building capacity. Some of the most interesting developments recently have been designs of school systems by teams of experts who will sell the instructional model to the schools and help the schools adopt the model. These models are supposedly based on research and are proven to work. Adoption of these models is spreading and the federal government is now supporting them. "Success for All" is one such model. There are fifteen or twenty variations, and there are more to come. So the idea is to build capacity by helping schools hook up with these external partners who know how to improve instruction.

A Multifaceted Approach to Solving Educational Problems

So these are the main thrusts that are being debated: accountability, changing governance, and capacity. I want to make several key points about them. First of all, they are by no means mutually exclusive; and, in my opinion, they have to go together. There is no point in talking about accountability if people don't have the capacity to respond. We actually have a research project in my center that's called "When Accountability Knocks, Is Anyone Home?" All our research on accountability is showing that the bonuses and the sanctions can get people's attention; but people won't be able to improve instruction if they don't know how to do it. That only makes sense, but you don't hear much discussion about this problem by politicians.

Politicians say that if you set up choice and charters, everybody will compete. Well, what if public schools don't know how to improve instruction in order to compete? And how much do the people starting charter schools know about good instruction? So it's not a question of just getting the incentives right; people have to have the capacity to respond to the incentives.

We need combinations of these approaches. There is no panacea. There is no magic bullet. If a public official asks what to do about education, the answer is: lots of things. It is tempting to think that a simple administrative change will make a big difference. But it won't.

Improving instruction is the core of improvement in education. If what is taught doesn't change, if teaching methods don't change, there is little reason to expect student learning to improve. This is not to say that instruction is the only factor, because, if kids are hungry and cold, they can't learn either. But, if teaching doesn't change, why should we expect students to learn more?

One question to ask about any reform concerns the link between this reform and instruction. What is the theory of action? If you ask yourself that, you would be amazed at how many reforms people propose, from the president on down, that don't include a clear explanation of how they are linked to improving instruction.

Who Has Responsibility?

All the debates about education are taking place in a setting where people are also questioning the intergovernmental allocation of authority around schooling. Historically, states had the constitutional responsibility for education but they delegated it to the localities. Over the past twenty years, states have increased their roles significantly. The standards movement is the latest manifestation. States are tightening regulations, increasing high school graduation requirements, increasing the amount of money they put in education, and assuming a much more powerful role. The federal government's role has traditionally been marginal and targeted. It has been for issues of national need like special math and science programs. Or we have had federal attention directed specifically at issues like equity or equality of access. Most K–12 federal spending is a large program called Title I, which goes to states and schools and districts on the basis of poverty. The higher the poverty rate, the more money they get. It is to help children who are disadvantaged. So federal money has always been targeted for those needs.

I think in the next Congress we will see a substantial increase in education funding. The debate will be over whether federal aid should be less targeted. The Republican position will be to say that educational policy is not a federal issue; the federal government can provide money for education, but should send it out to states and localities. Let the schools, who know best, decide how to spend it. The Democrats will say, if we send federal money without any strings, states and localities might sometimes spend it in ways that promote inequality. Federal money has been much more equalizing than local money—research has shown this to be true. Also, federal money tends to get to the classroom much more than the state and local money, which is also used for debt service, transportation, and so on. Democrats will say, don't just send the money to the states, send it with some guidance. Keep it targeted on poverty, keep it focused on improving instruction, say it has to be used for professional development tied to standards. Don't just let it be used for anything. We'll just have fifteen thousand variations and no significant improvement. That will be the debate that goes on in the next Congress.

I think we are poised to see an expansion in the federal role even if only in the percentage of funding for education that comes from the federal government. Inevitably, more federal money means more national direction. We are inching there with the national model standards. Every time you look at the international results, people say other countries have more national agreement on what to teach, and they point to how much better they are doing. I think we are going to see some increase in the federal role. If not federal, then national, meaning national independent bodies, or professional bodies, or national agreements among the states.

An Investment Mentality Toward Educational Policy

Another point I want to make is that we have a crying need for evaluation in education. So, across all these reforms, one of the big problems is we don't know enough. Less than 1 percent of total spending on education goes into research. Private firms put 7 percent into R&D. We make all kinds of reforms and we don't learn enough about what works and what doesn't. We must change that.

Finally, across all the reforms, I think it is really important to try and keep an investment mentality. There is a wide range of things to be done; we need to look at each effort as an investment in an overall policy and evaluate each new program on the basis of how it fits this policy—much as you are supposed to look at a new investment and consider how it fits into your whole portfolio. Following an investment mentality is the best way to accomplish our goals.

Improving Public Safety in Cities

Thomas M. Seamon

Before we can talk about what governments can do to improve public safety in cities, we need to consider first how current concepts of policing developed, and the changes that are taking place in policing right now.

How Current Police Procedures Evolved

Policing in the United States is primarily local. We have over 17,000 municipal or county police departments, and they affect the lives of citizens much more than state police and federal government agencies. I have discussed American policing with a lot of police officials from around the world, and sometimes it is difficult for them to understand that our decentralized policing system works far better than it ought to on paper. We obviously don't have a national police force, although some people suspect the Federal Bureau of Investigation (FBI) would like to become one; but the FBI is not the true national police force found in many other countries.

There has been a constant evolution since 1900 in the way that the United States polices itself. There are sometimes articles in the general press that describe a golden age of law enforcement, where the friendly beat officer walked down the street, knew all the children, and knew all the residents. Life was great in the United States and we didn't have today's crime problems.

The good old days never existed. The police, unfortunately, were brutal. There was a lot of corruption, and police were used by the government to make sure that immigrants and other people in the lower economic groups were kept in line and that order was maintained at any cost. There certainly was very little in the way of training: The selection of police officers was mainly by patronage. In fact, in Philadelphia it was widely known that if you wanted to become a police officer, you gave your ward leader $500 and you had a job. There was no scientific supervision or education for the police.

From about 1900 to the 1930s, while the police were largely uneducated and untrained, they did provide other services besides what people today think of as law enforcement. They were a kind of community watch; in some cities, police actually manned shelters and soup kitchens, and in crowded inner cities a lot of informal dispute resolution was done by the cop on the beat.

The 1930s saw the rise of civil service standards for hiring and education and for the formation and conduct of police organizations, a process interrupted by World War II. After the war it became accepted that the way to clean up corruption and to control large municipal police forces was to model police as paramilitary organizations. By the end of the 1950s and all through the 1960s and 1970s, policing had been transformed by what is called the professional policing model. If you have ever seen the old TV show *Dragnet,* with Jack Webb, you have seen this model police officer— "just the facts, ma'am." It actually started on the West Coast, in Los Angeles and other cities, and then moved slowly east. It took police officers off the beat and put them in automobiles with what was then high technology: two-way radios. It also redefined the policeman as a law-enforcement officer to the exclusion of other functions besides crime suppression, such as crime prevention, order maintenance, and service to the community.

The new model did improve police forces but removed a lot of the good aspects of the contact between the police and the citizens they served. The professionals knew best, so they really didn't need input from the community. The police would decide what was best for the residents, and they would then enforce the rules.

In the early and mid-1960s there were large-scale civil disturbances in

American cities, some of them sparked by racial problems, some of them sparked by other problems, but the scale of rioting and civil disturbances had not been seen since the Civil War. Responding to these riots further paramilitarized urban police, as they started to think about how they would control large groups of people who were disorderly. They worked out some of their methods in conjunction with the military forces. Then there were the anti–Vietnam War demonstrations in the late 1960s, which further militarized the police.

During and after Vietnam, crime started to skyrocket in the United States. No one really understands what produced this disturbing trend. One explanation is simple: demographics. Most crimes are committed by males between the ages of 14 and 24. That is the most crime-prone group, not just in the United States but in almost any culture. As the baby boom cohort reached these ages, crime rates went up.

It also became clear that whatever the police were doing to control crime wasn't working, because crime continued to go up. Citizens certainly weren't happy with the services they were getting from the police, nor were they happy about the relations that they had with police departments.

The concept called "team policing" grew up on the West Coast around 1984–85, starting in Los Angeles and San Jose, and once again, influenced police departments across the country. The idea was to take a section of the city and give it to a group of police officers and detectives of various ranks and functions and have them be responsible for this part of the community twenty-four hours a day, seven days a week. It was up to that group of police officers, police supervisors, and detectives to decide what hours and days of the week they should work and how they should coordinate their activities to provide services to the citizens. Team policing never really caught on. It was a good idea, but in implementation, because of problems with supervision, it wasn't as successful as people had hoped it would be. But out of these experiments with team policing, which was area based, came the real beginning of the philosophy of community policing in this country.

Anyone who reads the general press knows about community policing, about storefront police stations and how we've come full circle now and have taken officers out of their patrol cars and put them back on the beat. If you take 100 police chiefs and ask them if they practice community policing, at least 90 of them will say they do. It's like Mom, apple pie, and the American flag; nobody can be against community policing. But then if you ask the same chiefs how they implement community policing in their city, many of them will be hard pressed to tell you. They may tell you that they opened up the storefront police station, or they put some officers on foot patrol, but they miss the point, they miss the point entirely. What community policing is actually about is that the police should, first of all, regard the citizens as their customers, not as people that should be controlled. They should also ask their customers what kind of services they want.

Changes in policing come in cycles—one idea may catch hold for five to ten years, and then suddenly may be discredited and followed by a new form of policing. We're probably in the transition phase right now, from community policing to something else. It is not clear what this something else will be called, but it starts with community policing and adds what is called zero tolerance, plus some powerful new technology. Everyone is looking at New York City and what happened when Rudolph Giuliani took over as mayor and William Bratton became police commissioner.

Just before Giuliani and Bratton took office, the city put about 3,000 new police officers into the community and basically said, "Do good, liaison with the community, put community groups together." Well, these poor folks weren't trained for such tasks; they didn't have experience, and so they spent several years wandering around the streets of New York City. Only a small minority was successful in helping to organize communities to help themselves against crime. Bratton brought all those people back into more traditional policing roles, but then took volunteers, took older more experienced officers who would be more comfortable with and more experienced in working with the community, and put them out on the streets in a community policing role.

The police were confident for years that they knew what citizens wanted; they wanted the police to set their priorities to control the most serious crimes, like murder and robbery. But when the police finally sat down and started to talk to citizens and community groups face to face, the citizens told the police

> Well, yes, we think it is important that you catch murderers; but, thank goodness, I haven't been murdered, and no one in my family has been murdered. You think it is very important to catch robbers, but, thank goodness, I've never been robbed, my cousin was several years ago but he wasn't hurt bad and it's certainly impor-

tant—but you know what really bothers me? When I go to the corner, to the 7-Eleven, to buy milk, there's a group of teenagers that stands on the corner and when I go by, they make remarks, and in fact, I don't even go to the 7-Eleven any more at night, I only go in the daytime. I used to take the subway to work, but it's smelly. There's a scary looking man on the platform when I go down and he's always asking me for a quarter and he's never threatened me but I am not sure if I don't give him the quarter what he'll do. There are also teenagers with loud radios, so I don't use the subway anymore.

Citizens need to feel safe and comfortable in urban areas or they will relocate their homes and businesses out of the city. As citizens make their personal assessment of urban public safety, the perception of crime is as important as the reality of crime. A city government may be able to demonstrate through crime statistics that the level of reported crime is declining or is low compared to other urban areas; however, people make decisions about safety based on the environment they experience daily.

In their daily commute to their offices, if workers see dirty littered streets, step over sleeping homeless on sidewalks, and are approached by numerous panhandlers, they will translate this disorder as crime. This type of streetscape gives the impression that government is not in charge. The experience is chaotic and may people translate this chaos into danger.

Eventually if this disorder continues, without the police and other governmental agencies taking corrective action, businesses will make decisions to relocate out of the city. If an executive has a highly valued assistant, and she complains each day that she is afraid to come to work in the city; her input will weigh heavily on future decisions to relocate the company.

New York City decided on a policy of zero tolerance for any type of crime: loud radios, drinking in public, very low level drug dealing on corners, disorderly crowds, everything of this nature; and they started to find out that if these types of crimes are addressed, it will bring down the crime rate for more serious offenses. However, it is not just zero tolerance that has had a phenomenal effect on serious crimes in the city. The police started using Computer Crime Analysis in a system called COMSTAT.

The police always kept statistics, but usually the information was three to six months old before it got into the hands of the people making operational decisions on the street. What New York City did was to start bringing in all the managers every week and giving them information that was only twenty-four hours old. Say captain, this is what is happening in your district, what are you doing about it? Do you know what the problem is? And then there was the novel concept too that the commander who didn't respond or perform well as the manager would be removed. So there are a lot of things working together to bring about what's happening in New York City.

Another aspect was to ask the police how could they handle their workload better if they looked at the city as a series of communities. For instance, instead of going to the same burglar alarm 250 times a year, take a little extra time, meet with the owner of the building, and help the owner fix the alarm so you don't have to go there anymore. Or imagine a home where there is a dysfunctional couple; let's say the husband's an alcoholic who comes home every Friday night and beats his wife. So, the police are out there fifty times a year. Take some time, revisit that location when the husband isn't drunk, sit both parties down, and try to get them in touch with some other social services so that the wife can receive counseling and support or even go into a shelter for battered women or so that they can, perhaps, get their marriage back on track. The main thing is to stop going to that house fifty times a year—if you multiply that example by tens of thousands of calls, you begin to see how the police could free themselves up to provide the kind of services the citizens want.

Crime statistics have been improving in major cities that have adopted new policies, but there is some discussion of how much of that is due to demographics and how much of that is due to the efforts of the police. One thing is clear, police methods are going to continue to evolve and change. Two important trends right now are relationships between the public police and private security forces, and the use of powerful new technologies, such as computers in police vehicles and closed circuit television to monitor locations.

New Trends in Policing

Public police generally look down on private security forces, but over the past ten years employment in private security in this country has been growing at the rate of about 10 to 12 percent a year. At the same time, especially over the past five years, employment in public policing has remained relatively stagnant. Today there are almost three people employed in private security for every person employed in public law enforcement. About 750,000 people are involved in law enforcement in local, state, and federal police agencies. Over 2 million are employed as security guards, as guards in private prisons, in the alarm business, or in private organizations that have much more sophisticated capabilities than the police to investigate complex computer frauds—high technology–related crimes. You could say that there is probably a sum that the country is willing to spend on public safety and what is happening is that police are losing their market share to private organizations. Extrapolating this trend into the future, one could envision a possible scenario in which the public police lose their dominance of the public safety market to private providers.

Imagine a world in which businesspeople leave home in the morning to commute to work. They live in a gated community protected by private security. The public police rarely patrol the community; they only come in when called. The office complex is secured by alarm systems, access control systems, and closed circuit television security systems and is patrolled by private security officers. These people in business have little use for the public police. Because of this, they vote down bond issues that would support funding of the public police. With decreased funding the police service deteriorates, confirming the notion that private security is the better service.

This scenario is analogous to what actually exists in the health care system in America. Everyone who can afford private health care, either by personal wealth or by insurance, utilizes private doctors. Only the poor, especially the urban poor, utilize the public health system. Reflecting on this model, one could imagine the public police becoming the police of the poor.

Many police authorities discount this scenario by relying on the fact that the public police are exclusively granted arrest powers and other official powers from the state. This situation could change quickly if state legislatures simply granted limited official powers to private security organizations.

The same situation could also be perceived as a great opportunity for the police to augment their effectiveness by working with private security. I have been advising my colleagues to get over the fact that we are losing our market share and cooperate with private security now. The president may talk about programs to put 100,000 more police officers on the rolls throughout the country, but these federal funds pay 75 percent of salary for the first year, 50 percent of salary the second year, and 25 percent the third year. Then the agency must pick up the full cost. A police department may get a hundred extra police officers now, but after a few years their staffing will go back down because they don't have the permanent funding.

In Philadelphia, the Center City District is a public–private partnership. There is a surcharge on commercial properties; the money that is raised goes chiefly for two things: supplemental street and sidewalk cleaning and extra public-security officers on the streets. They are not police officers, they are private security, but they are performing a public function. And I like that they are called community service representatives. They are a combination of a paid town watch and a public concierge. They are in uniforms, they have radio communications with the police, they are not armed, and they don't have power of arrest. They are out there to help people, whatever their problem is, whether they are lost and need directions, or their cars are broken down, or they are coming out of office buildings late at night and need escorts to their cars. The representatives may also report a crime or impending crime conditions that they see.

I was the police commander of Center City when they started the Center City District. We decided to put a police station into the District and to have city police officers work very closely, side by side, with these private security officers—something that had never been done in this country. At first the police officers said they couldn't work with the security officers. But we actually involved the police in the initial training of the community service representatives and, more importantly, we forced the police to work with them. When all else fails in the police department, the person in command can say, Do it because I told you to. What we found was that within a very short time all the animosity dissipated. Both groups realized that the others were just human beings; they occupied the same office space and shared local facilities, and they found they could work together very successfully.

We have found the same dynamic operates here at the University of Pennsylvania. We have the contract security officers out on the streets with the police officers. Although there was initial animosity and suspicion and tension, these obstacles were overcome.

The second big issue the police are facing is how to adapt to new technology—computers in police vehicles, using computers to analyze crime, automatic fingerprint identification systems—the technology is mind-boggling. Many police forces either don't have the money to invest in these technologies or haven't yet understood their power to change the way they do business.

At the University of Pennsylvania, the University Council recently authorized closed circuit television monitoring of streets. We are putting cameras on public streets that will help us monitor and police those areas. The kind of criminals who are often repeat offenders, such as robbers, car thieves, burglars, and vandals who plague urban areas, can be videotaped during their first offense, enabling quick, successful investigations and arrests. Obviously we try to prevent as much crime as possible. But when someone slips past us, video footage of a crime in progress makes a profound impression on judge and jury, leading to high conviction rates. I think the use of cameras will have as big an effect on policing as the introduction of the two-way radio did seventy years ago. There is not a police chief today who can imagine running a police department without a radio. As we install cameras, we will want to restructure the department, but it isn't yet clear how they will affect staffing, deployment, and operational procedures.

Recommendations

1. Generate national standards for police training and development.
The first thing I would propose would be national standards for the recruitment, training, and development of police. The quality of police in this country is extremely variable, because the standards vary. Although the state governments develop standards, they still vary from state to state. The number of hours police need in initial training to get certified and have a license vary tremendously. In Pennsylvania, the initial period of training before an officer is out on the streets is four months, yet the City of Philadelphia trains for seven months. In Germany, training takes two years. There are also no national standards for measurement of competence, both of individual officers and of whole police departments. Certainly, national standards would be a way to ensure the quality of police services that are delivered in this country. Federal grants could be contingent on each state adopting the national standard.

2. Target federal aid to the areas that need it most.
My second suggestion calls for regular, ongoing federal and/or state funding to supplement police budgets in the urban areas that need help the most. Some 35 percent of the crimes in the United States are committed in fifty urban jurisdictions. Policing these urban environments requires efforts on a completely different scale from that of rural policing or suburban policing. The areas that bear the brunt of the social problems in this country need special federal support. In the United Kingdom, the Home Office funds 50 percent of all police budgets. In the United States, we have always been afraid that central funding will lead to national police, but it puts an unfair burden on the citizens of big cities to pay for all the extra services the urban areas need. This financial support could also be tied in to the adoption of national standards for training and evaluating competence.

3. Develop a new strategy for handling the drug problem.
Another priority is the need for a new national strategy for handling the drug problem. I spent many years in the "War on Drugs." We lost it. Enforcement hasn't worked. We put more people in jail than any other Western country and most of them are in there because they are either low-level drug dealers or they have used drugs, or both; there's a big overlap. Many people who have a dependency on hard drugs are going to be involved in the supply of drugs to support their own habits. Our jails are so full of these people that we have no room for serious criminals. And yet there has been no effect on drug use and drug related crimes.

I don't favor legalization, however. What I think we need to do is treat drug abuse as a medical problem. Although we don't decriminalize the use of drugs, the major emphasis and resources should go for a joint effort between the medical community and the police. Our only chance is to make drug use socially unacceptable, so that people will want to give up their addiction. The pattern to follow is the great job that has been done on smoking. The number of people who smoke now is down drastically from what it was five years ago. The same effort can and should be exerted for other drugs. Why are some people much more susceptible to drug addiction than others? What is it that addicts are seeking, despite their knowledge of the destructive consequences? Are there other ways to give drug users what they need, without addiction and the devastating side effects? The history of the past twenty to twenty-five years in policing has been totally distorted by the war on drugs. We need to get the medical community involved in trying to change social behavior with regard to drugs.

4. Institute a national safety code.

The last recommendation I want to make is on the prevention side. We spend a lot of money to arrest people and put them in jail. In the end we would do much better to prevent crime and alter the conditions that lead to crime. The fire and building codes in this country have grown up over the years into a very complex series of regulations. They are very well observed, and they have made a big difference in both the incidence of fires and the ability to save people and control fires if they do break out.

Fire and safety regulations in buildings determine whether there can be a lock on the door, what kind of hallways are needed, how many exits are necessary for the building, and so on. These requirements are nonnegotiable. People are not even allowed to enter a new building until the government comes, inspects, and determines that it meets the code. We should start thinking about doing the same thing for security and safety in buildings and even outdoor public spaces. Designers and builders of facilities or public spaces should be required to adhere to certain minimum security codes. There has been enough research into making buildings and places safer that we know how to prevent a significant amount of crime, instead of chasing it around. It would be fairly simple to comply with security codes, and it certainly would be less expensive than complying with fire codes, which are universally complied with now. Why this idea has never taken hold at the police end of the spectrum of public safety, I don't know. We certainly have the system of federal standards for fire safety and state and local building laws and codes to use as the model for public safety codes.

C h a p t e r   9

Welfare Reform, Reproductive Reform, or Work Reform?

Roberta Rehner Iversen

U.S. Social Welfare Policy in the Twentieth Century: Values and Myths

Social policy is essentially values in action—the ways in which social values about the welfare of the populace are translated into laws and programs. However, in order to have appropriate laws and programs, social values need to be based on reality rather than on myth. Throughout U.S. history, social welfare policy has had a strong mythic base: In particular, that America is a land of opportunity for all. Work opportunity is believed to be unlimited by social or political structure and universally available. Race, gender, marital status, or socioeconomic position at birth should not affect opportunity. Consequently, if opportunity is not perceived or utilized, the individual must be at fault.

As a result, only a few persons who were poor and unemployed have historically been categorized as "deserving" rather than "undeserving," thus meriting extraordinary supports from the people at large (i.e., the federal government) to ensure their well-being or "welfare." The ideology of individual responsibility and the primacy of the work ethic intersected to feed the myth of opportunity, to the particular detriment of marginalized sectors of society such as women and people of color. Compounding this myth, the composition of the labor force in postindustrial America was historically constructed along lines of gender and race. Men's primacy in the public sphere of work was balanced by women's relegation to the private sphere of home and family. This mythic construction ignored the realities of race and class, in that women of color have had high historic rates of labor force participation and working-class men and women have never had the choice not to work. For most of our recent history, social welfare policy reflected the mythic construction of "proper" gender and work roles.

Since "proper" gender roles were assigned according to the presumption of two-parent families, the social and economic needs of the "single mother" and how to define her role have been a central focus of social welfare policy for at least a century. The panoply of terms for the female marital and reproductive role through the twentieth century, such as "single mothers," "unmarried mothers," "never-married mothers," "deserted wives," and "out-of-wedlock childbirth," illustrates the normative expectation of marriage. Nevertheless, social welfare legislation did not overtly centerpiece marriage as a solution to economic needs until 1996. As numbers on welfare grew over the decades, the term "welfare" changed from one that denoted a system of social and economic services for the general good to a term that denoted a system of services that engineered the reproductive and work behavior of poor individuals.

Mother's or Widow's Pensions (1910–1935)

Men's early deaths and family desertion resulted in rising numbers of single mothers in the last part of the nineteenth century and early decades of the twentieth, especially among the poor. In response, state and local governments instituted aid in the form of "mother's or widow's pensions" that were specifically designed to foster the ability of the deserted or widowed mother to stay at home to care for her children, emphasizing that women's proper "labor" was mothering. As welfare historian Linda Gordon noted, the "widow discourse" distinguished the "worthy" single mothers from the "unworthy," those deserted, from those bearing "illegitimate" children. Ironically, this feminist-initiated discourse inadvertently spotlighted marital status. To ensure that recipients were among the worthy, welfare administrators scrutinized recipients' morality, restricted citizenship, and instituted investigative "men in the house" and "midnight raid" practices.

In reality, the level of aid seldom sufficed to keep these mothers out of the labor force, but the myth of support was perpetuated and marriage was not promoted as a solution to need. Moreover, before the mid-twentieth century, the meanings of single motherhood were shaped by the experiences of white urban native and immigrant women rather than African American women who were still predominantly rural. It was only with increases of African American women in northern cities that "welfare" assumed a black face.

Aid to Dependent Children (ADC) (1935–1962)

Massive poverty and economic need during the Great Depression rendered mother's pensions inadequate. As a result, Aid to Dependent Children (ADC), part of the Social Security Act of 1935, marked the first federal involvement in welfare policy. Following the pattern of aid set by mother's pensions, ADC still allowed women to stay home and raise their children. In this way ADC was a maternalist policy, one that fostered the value that raising children was an important social responsibility. ADC was also a feminist policy in its availability to all women, which theoretically reduced their economic dependence on male providers. At the same time, because the Depression caused high levels of unemployment among men, women's participation in the labor force was strongly discouraged.

In reality, ADC was a means-tested program, underfunded and intended as a temporary solution to need. ADC assumed the primacy of marriage. Policymakers expected that other, more universal social insurance entitlement programs, such as unemployment and old age survivor's insurance for unemployed and retired breadwinners, would cover the economic needs of dependent women and children, ultimately obviating their need for federal financial assistance. Accordingly, in a critical change from mother's pensions, ADC was given only to children and not to the mothers. Society's growing ambivalence about which women were and were not deserving of aid was exemplified by the ADC eligibility requirement of a "suitable home." As Linda Gordon noted in the passage cited earlier, the presence of a man in the house or the birth of an illegitimate child made the home unsuitable. This requirement also allowed the racial prejudices of welfare investigators to influence determination of "suitability." Thus, although neither unmarried motherhood nor divorce was overt in welfare law or discourse at this time, social assumptions about proper motherhood and mechanisms designed to control women's sexuality were now codified at the federal level.

Aid to Families with Dependent Children (AFDC) (1962–1996)

The decades following World War II saw booming economic prosperity, steady increases in women's labor force participation, new reproductive technology, changing norms about marriage and divorce, and the discordant recognition that poverty existed amid plenty, especially among women and people of color. The civil rights, welfare rights, and feminist movements in particular illuminated the chasm between America's myth of opportunity and the realities of social and economic disparities according to race and gender. Accordingly, federal funding for ADC was expanded in the mid-1950s to give both financial and social service support to the parent of a dependent child. Under the Public Welfare Amendments of 1962, the name of ADC was changed to Aid to Families with Dependent Children (AFDC).

Accompanying this new provision of social, educational, and vocational services in the context of a strong economy, work as the antidote to poverty emerged as a policy emphasis. AFDC legislation now measured the goal of "strengthened family life" in terms of recipients' material rather than maternal success, as was the case in the earlier welfare policies. Distinguishing the causes of poverty from unemployment and economic depression that formed the basis of ADC, President Kennedy's Message to Congress on Public Welfare in 1962 framed poverty primarily in relation to personal characteristics and work capabilities: "Some are in need because they are untrained for work—some because they cannot work, because they are too young or too old, blind, or crippled." In short, public welfare must be increasingly directed toward prevention and rehabilitation—offering the total resources of the community to help less fortunate citizens help themselves. Family strengthening was the ideological and instrumental goal of AFDC and work was the key to strengthening family life. For the first time, the "proper" women's role was worker as well as mother. Since 86 percent of children still lived with two parents at this time, promotion of marriage was still not central on the policy horizon.

In the twenty-four years following the formulation of AFDC the marital status and reproductive behaviors of poor women became a preeminent societal and policy concern. Changing norms about sexuality, marriage, and unwed motherhood, increased urban poverty, and limited work opportunity among poor men resulted in rising numbers of female-headed households. Moreover, AFDC limited eligibility to one-parent families, indirectly fostering single parenthood over two-parent families among the poor. By 1990, 34 percent of one-parent, female-headed households were poor and at least as many more were classified as near-poor. Worse yet, over half of black and Hispanic female-headed families lived in poverty. At the same time, women's participation in the labor market increased from 30 percent in 1960 to 69 percent in 1990.

Nevertheless, rhetoric about an "epidemic of teenage pregnancy and childbearing," "the problem that hasn't gone away," and ultimately "family values," obscured the reality that spiraling welfare costs were due to the intersection of extremely complex elements such as changing demography, economic recessions, global competition in production, and rising unemployment coupled with an increasingly conservative federal government. Ignoring this complexity, the inflammatory rhetoric fueled and focused taxpayer discontent on women's work and reproductive behaviors and roles as the cause of rising costs.

Accordingly, this quarter-century of welfare policy was accompanied not only by expanded social services and counseling programs, but also by a proliferation of legislated work programs: AFDC-UP for unemployed parents in 1964, the Work Incentive Program (WIN) in 1967, and the Job Opportunities and Basic Skills (JOBS) Training Program in 1988 that sought to "provide support and foster personal responsibility." Under AFDC-UP and WIN, work was encouraged but not broadly mandated. State departments of welfare could choose whether or not to require recipient work participation. Under JOBS, welfare recipients were mandated for the first time to find work or be subject to sanctions. The JOBS policy also required states to move designated percentages off welfare and into work. Still, JOBS exempted mothers with children under age 3 (or age 1, by state option) from mandatory participation. Only about half the adult caseload was expected to participate. Thus, despite increasing emphasis on work, single mothers' roles of parent and/or worker were preserved.

At the same time, single mothers' reproductive behavior was under vitriolic attack from an increasingly conservative populace and government. Despite the landmark abortion legislation in 1973 (*Roe v. Wade*), theoretically freeing women to control their own reproductive careers, subsequent legislative limitations meant that poor women in particular were less able to decide their futures. However, since reproductive issues were handled by departments of health and human services, and public assistance issues by departments of public welfare, in the waning years of AFDC, reproductive and welfare rights remained administratively separate. Continuous efforts to limit the scope of reproductive policy and practices during the 1980s, together with rising welfare rolls, rising social welfare expenditures, severe cutbacks in social services, and periods of economic recession, paved the way for overt linkage of welfare use, reproduction, and marital behavior in the major welfare reform legislation of the mid-1990s.

Welfare Reform as Reproductive Policy: PRWORA

The Personal Responsibility and Work Opportunity Reconciliation Act (PRWORA) of 1996, commonly known as "welfare reform," replaced the federal AFDC program with a block grant to the states called Temporary Assistance to Needy Families (TANF). PRWORA essentially moved responsibility for the unemployed poor from the federal government back to the states, where it had originated nearly a century earlier. Notably, the ideological rationale as presented in the first two and a half pages of PRWORA moved marriage and control of reproductive behavior from being absent or a covert subtext to overt foreground. Congressional opinion in these pages stated that, in the words of the legislation, "marriage is the foundation of a successful society. Prevention of out-of-wedlock pregnancy and reduction in out-of-wedlock birth are very important Government interests and . . . the policy is intended to address the crisis [of out-of-wedlock pregnancies, births, and welfare dependency]." The next section of PRWORA declares that the specific purpose of TANF block grants is to give states flexibility in operating a program designed "to end the dependence of needy parents on government benefits by promoting job preparation, work, and marriage . . . to prevent and reduce the incidence of out-of-wedlock pregnancies and establish annual numerical goals for preventing and reducing the incidence of these pregnancies . . . and to encourage the formation and maintenance of two-parent families."

If ever there were a frantic message to right the inadvertent support for nonmarital households promoted by AFDC and return to the "traditional family structure," PRWORA is it. Notably, by 1990 only 13 percent of families compared to almost 60 percent in 1950 were constituted in the "traditional" form: two parents with children wherein one parent is the wage earner and the other is at home with the children. "Nontraditional" family forms are casualties—or benefits depending on one's point of view—of such historical influences as the feminist movement, civil rights legislation, rising incidence of divorce, changes in reproductive technology and legislation, increased rates of women's employment, shifts in the structure of the labor market with attendant increases in un- and underemployment among (formerly marriageable) young men and people of color, and postponement of marriage or devaluation of marriage as an institution.

In response, it is certainly not accidental that "personal responsibility" precedes "work opportunity" in the title of PRWORA. Essentially, the goal of the act is reduction in unwed childbearing and consequent termination of public assistance. The primary means to this goal is marriage; the secondary means is employment. Inclusion of both solutions tacitly acknowledges that women on welfare are not likely to find jobs with wages that will support a family; hence, marriage with its attendant two-person wage attainment is the more likely road to economic self-sufficiency. Obviously, more structural solutions such as expanded training and skills, career ladders with supplementary supports, and development of more jobs at family-wage and benefit levels could perpetuate unmarried parenthood, and thus are replaced by marriage on the policy radar screen.

The PRWORA is a highly controversial social policy—supported strongly by generally conservative state governors, the general public, and a Republican-dominated Congress, and opposed equally strongly by children's advocates, liberal policy analysts, and social service organizations. States who view the policy as enlightened enforcement of America's work ethic have reported precipitous drops in their welfare rolls of at least 30 percent on average, although many analysts attribute this drop to the strong economy rather than to the new policy. Advocacy groups who view the policy as coercive, draconian, racist, and sexist have reported equally great failures. Children's poverty increased during the 1990s, even among children in two-parent families, TANF policy implementation was uneven and harmful to work-program participants, and increased reports of food affordability issues coincided with perplexing drops in use of the Food

Stamp program. Only two in five families eligible for Food Stamps took part in the program in 1999. Despite the fact that states are supposed to collect data and report quarterly on job attachment activities under TANF, levels of technological development are insufficient to reveal what happened to those who left the rolls. Basically, no one knows for sure why so many women left the welfare rolls, where they went, where they are now, or most important, how they and their dependent children are doing economically. Some research reports that no more than one-quarter of former recipients left welfare for employment. In reality, we do not know whether individuals have left the welfare rolls because of employment, marriage, or sanction.

Welfare Reform as Work Reform

Nature of the TANF Program

Two critical differences pertain to TANF assistance compared to its federal predecessor, AFDC. First, adults in families receiving TANF assistance must participate in work activities after receiving assistance for twenty-four months, or earlier if states decree. In fact, most states impose a work activity requirement immediately upon TANF enrollment. Second, mandatory time limits now exist in all states resulting in a maximum of five years of allowable TANF assistance over a person's lifetime. Although 20 percent of welfare caseloads may qualify for "hardship" exemption from this five-year limit, no guidelines for this categorical exemption have been formulated to date.

States now have broad latitude to design critical features of their welfare policy such as recipient criteria, time limits, and exemption guidelines as well as its overall aims. Accordingly, almost half the states have imposed family cap provisions limiting assistance to children born before TANF regulations went into effect. The other half have not. States can also decide whether or not federal exemption from the five-year time limit applies to their work requirements. Regarding aims, the purpose of Pennsylvania's basic welfare law before spring 1996 was "to promote the welfare and happiness of all the people of the Commonwealth by providing public assistance." After spring 1996, Pennsylvania's version of TANF, Act No. 1996-35 (Act 35) intended "to promote the self-sufficiency of all the people in the Commonwealth."

Most interestingly, although PRWORA rhetoric emphasizes marriage and personal responsibility, TANF programs are focused on work. In line with the incremental emphasis on work over training and social supports in welfare policy of the past several decades, "work first" is the directive given by most state governments as they implement TANF. At the same time, PRWORA also directs every state to formulate an "Individual Responsibility Plan" that generally identifies only the recipient's personal responsibility for work. Of all fifty states' plans, only Pennsylvania's "Agreement of Mutual Responsibility" acknowledges the need for both programs and recipients to take responsibility for employment efforts.

Snags and Limitations in TANF Policy Implementation

In actual practice, implementation of TANF welfare-to-work programs has been a critical problem for assistance recipients and program personnel alike. My field research in Philadelphia-area welfare-to-work programs found massive delays in program start-ups and strained program operations that were due in part to faulty policy logic, organizational and personnel incompetence, and inadequate coordination between and within funding, referral, program, and employer organizations. Such barriers to welfare recipients' work efforts occurred regularly but received little public or research attention compared to the focus on their skill and attitudinal barriers, and the wage and retention barriers in the service sector jobs they obtained.

"Quick attachment" policy logic is faulty in its over-reliance on human and social capital concepts and its inattention to the amount of time necessary for both individuals and organizations to ensure the welfare-to-work transition. At policy onset, the main conduit for TANF policy implementation, the Pennsylvania Department of Public Welfare (DPW), was technologically unable to track individuals on or when they left the welfare rolls. The DPW initially predicted there would be more demand for service in Philadelphia than the existing capacity could supply. After the first year of implementation, it appeared that the supply of programs exceeded participant demand. By spring 1999, 15,000 TANF recipients were expected to enroll in programs sponsored by the city's welfare-to-work system, Greater Philadelphia Works, but only 7,995 actually did. State tracking capacity was unable to explain this disconnect.

The Department of Public Welfare was also technologically unable to identify essential recipient characteristics among those remaining on the rolls, which meant that the primary referral agencies, County Assistance Offices (CAOs), could not generate the information needed by the implementing agencies to effect an appropriate match between a given client and a given service. As a result, the Philadelphia programs had difficulty recruiting sufficient participants, and similar difficulties have since been reported across the nation.

An interrelated cause of inappropriate referral and delayed enrollment stemmed from the fact that CAO staff who had been benefits administrators before TANF were expected to become work-program specialists in a short time period, without new training and without having appropriate educational backgrounds. The multiplicity of new roles under TANF is graphically illustrated by the array of new titles at the CAOs. Benefits administrators or eligibility workers have now become employment advisers, job developers, job coaches, and employment coordinators. In particular, eligibility workers are now expected to forge relationships with TANF recipients based on mutuality and reciprocity rather than on hierarchy and autonomy, as was the case under AFDC. Worse yet, perhaps confused by the profusion of new roles and functions, CAO workers frequently did not give work-program participants information about their continued eligibility for Food Stamp and Medicaid benefits or childcare and transportation allowances. At the state level, the DPW erroneously cut off 30,000 parents from childcare allowances they were eligible for, resulting in many work-program dropouts before the benefits were reinstated several months later. These infractions compounded the penalty to TANF recipients of the time lost by inappropriate referral to job training programs.

Adding to program delays caused by the lack of recipient information, funding requirements, characteristics of TANF referrals, and welfare-to-work program eligibility requirements were frequently mismatched. For example, the funding guidelines of two nursing-related programs required targeting "hard to employ" individuals who, among other criteria, "require substance abuse treatment for employment." However, state legislation (PA—Act 14) prohibits persons actively using drugs or alcohol from either training or working as certified nursing assistants in nursing homes—precisely the jobs for which the programs were training participants. Because CAOs are not required to screen for substance use before sending TANF recipients to apply for jobs or training programs, some participants began both nursing-related programs only to find out three to six weeks later that their drug and alcohol test performance prohibited continuation in the program. As a result, the individuals' time and energy were wasted, months on TANF continued to build, and the program's resources were spent fruitlessly.

Most important, these implementation problems penalized TANF recipients severely as they tried to move from welfare to work, depleting their time-limited assistance as they waited for programs to start or found themselves in inappropriate programs. Notably, most of the problems could have been predicted and prevented through attention to the significant body of literature about policy implementation developed over the past twenty-five years.

Recommendations

1. Create a federal department of workforce development or workforce welfare. At the level of philosophy and ideology, "welfare" policy should be reconceptualized as "workforce development" or "workforce welfare," predicated on the vast body of social science knowledge that embeds poverty in systemic and economic changes and conditions rather than on the unsubstantiated mythology of unlimited opportunity. Instead of seeing poor people as morally derelict, we should see them as potential workers. Instead of viewing the labor force as the only valid site for compensated "work," at-home parenting and combinations of labor market and family labor could be eligible for wage subsidy or compensation. A true "workforce welfare" program would help women and men be wage earners and meet domestic labor obligations.

Change from a "welfare" to a "workforce" ideology could be made operational at the national level by restructuring federal provision of public assistance and employment support along the lines of how labor and welfare were linked in the first federal aid program, the Federal Emergency Relief Act (FERA) of 1933. Presently, public assistance and employment training are lodged in two separate departments—public assistance in the Office of Family Assistance in the Administration for Children and Families, U.S. Department of Health and Human Services, and employment in the U.S. Department of Labor. TANF is administered by departments of human services in some states and departments of labor in others. Ideally, income support and workforce development should be linked.

The Workforce Investment Act of 1998 (WIA) could easily provide the medium for such linkage. According to Labor Secretary Alexis Herman's introduction to the act, WIA's one-stop system is designed to provide a full menu of job training, education, and employment services at a single neighborhood location where all adults, veterans, dislocated workers, and youth can receive skills assessment services, information on employment opportunities, unemployment services, job search and placement assistance, and up-to-date information on job vacancies. Under the act, the Labor Department already partners with the Department of Education in order to fully address school-to-work concerns.

A further step would be for the Department of Labor to partner with— or absorb—the Office of Family Assistance in order to provide a seamless stream of assistance for the work efforts of welfare parents, below-poverty workers, and those needing particular training and supports to get, keep, and advance in living-wage jobs. Many aspects of the Workforce Investment Act are sufficiently similar to TANF policy requirements to suggest that partnership would be neither incongruent nor difficult to make operational. TANF Individual Responsibility Plans are much like the Memoranda of Understanding required by the one-stop centers. TANF currently addresses service needs at different levels: those who can exit the rolls for employment without help, those who need eight-week job search/job readiness assistance to find employment, and those who need more intensive skills training and support services. The Workforce Investment Act also mandates a similar continuum of services ranging from self-service activities, to staff-assisted activities such as computer use and job network access, to more intensive staff services such as counseling and referral to training and other support services. Under a workforce "umbrella," it seems likely that the employment needs of all community members can be met. In addition, a more positive—and appropriate—view of all individuals as potential workers would be promoted.

At state and local levels, recent structural changes in Wisconsin's state government might serve as a partial guide. Wisconsin reorganized programs for income support, vocational rehabilitation, unemployment, and employment and training into a single department—the Department of Workforce Development (DWD). The DWD funnels support funds to seventeen service delivery areas throughout the state to universally, rather than selectively, fund one-stop employment and training job centers serving both job seekers and employers with varying levels of service assistance.

2. Sustain the current level of federal funding.

Short of "ideal" ideological and structural change, policymakers must work to sustain the agreed-upon level of federal funding for TANF block grants, set and frozen for five years according to levels of assistance outlay in the early 1990s. Because welfare rolls plummeted before PRWORA took full effect and the general economy has been strong, most states currently experience unspent TANF fund balances. The federal government now wants to "borrow" these state surpluses. In fall 1999, the House Appropriations Labor/HHS Subcommittee approved an appropriations bill for FY2000 to rescind $3 billion in TANF funds, nearly the entire surplus amount, that it claims it will reallocate in FY2001. Such policies make poor people subsidize the government. Some of the unspent TANF funds are unliquidated obligations—funds that a state has committed to service providers but not yet expended. Further, research suggests that the states with the most-disadvantaged caseloads will require the greatest resources per recipient to ensure the success of their reforms. If funds are rescinded, state plans to make new investments in programs that help parents find and keep jobs, such as childcare and transportation allotments, would be inoperable, leaving those who are most vulnerable without sufficient supports to make a successful transition from welfare to work. In addition, since states have viewed their surplus funds as a "safety net" for all aspiring and new workers in case of economic downturn, governmental borrowing would obliterate such protection.

3. Continue expansion and monthly allotment of income supplements.

Recent expansions in the Earned Income Tax Credit (EITC) have significantly increased employment and reduced returns to welfare among single parents. In many cases, the EITC is a critical transition support for new or returning workers in expanding below-poverty wages to the level of sustainable income. House leadership proposed in fall 1999 that the EITC be refunded as one lump sum payment rather than in monthly installments. The upshot of such a change would be that low-income individuals would be denied an essential wage supplement monthly as they need it in order to further subsidize the government's investment use of EITC dollars throughout the year. If such a bill passes, policymakers must work to rescind it.

Moreover, if Congress really wants to foster marriage, penalty relief for EITC recipients who are married, or who get married, is also needed. At present, the EITC available to two single individuals is generally greater than the amount available to the same individuals if married. Equalization of the amount would obviate such penalty.

4. Accelerate use of the "$500 Million Fund."

A provision of the 1996 law de-linked TANF and Medicaid with resultant drops in Medicaid coverage that were larger than drops in the welfare rolls. This de-linkage, combined with the fact that few entry-level jobs offer health benefits, means that increasing numbers of parents and children are not covered by health insurance. A recent Center on Budget and Policy Priorities report drew attention to the fact that a total of $500 million in federal matching funds accompanied state TANF allotments to ensure continued Medicaid and Children's Health Insurance Program coverage among families no longer on welfare. The report also noted that on average, only 10 percent of the funds were spent by June 1999. Policymakers can be urged to accelerate use of the "$500 Million Fund" before it expires in Fall 2000 or restore it if it has already expired, but was not used because of administrative confusion. Among other uses, such as increased media outreach and improved tracking technology, such funds could be used to educate CAO staff about eligibility criteria and subsidize hiring of additional personnel.

5. Refine state policies on time limits and permanent exemptions.

TANF recipients should not be penalized for the kinds of delays caused by policy implementation outlined above, thus changes in the twenty-four- and sixty-month TANF time limits are another critical policy target. Retroactive elimination of the two-year penalty and extension of recipients' two- and five-year time limits by the number of months lost because of delays in program start-up or inappropriate referrals would be a place to start. Time limits should also be suspended until County Assistance Office personnel are professionally qualified to identify recipients' needs and refer them to appropriate programs and services, until training providers are fully funded and operative, and until the disconnect between program supply and TANF recipient demand is fully understood.

The development of "exemption" policies, not yet fully defined in most states, is also critical. A few temporary exemptions to the two-year time limit have been granted to TANF recipients with state-selected character-istics. In Pennsylvania for example, the Department of Public Welfare can allow exemption for full-time care of incapacitated relatives, victims of domestic violence, family under DHS supervision, or loss or turndown of job for "good cause." But these exemptions are dependent upon individ-ual CAO caseworker discretion—individuals already found limited in training and employment-related knowledge.

Moreover, despite state-set exemptions, the federal clock of sixty months keeps ticking. Thus a significant arena for policy attention is the refinement of exemption policy for the "final" five-year period. In particu-lar, a substantive definition rather than a blanket 20 percent ceiling for per-manent exemption from the five-year limits should be developed in line with findings about the interaction between individual needs and labor market characteristics emerging from welfare research. Further, as TANF policy now stands, even if an individual is "exempt" from the federal five-year cutoff, she may not be exempt from state work requirements. Thus efforts to unify state and federal exemption policies are indicated. States should also stop using caseload decline as a measure of welfare reform suc-cess. Instead, they should craft a success measure based on carefully col-lected data about job attachment and retention and wage and benefit lev-els, assessing increases or decreases over time.

6. Replace TANF with MOE funds.

States can replace some TANF funds with state Maintenance-of-Effort (MOE) funds when possible. TANF time limits apply only to work sup-ports defined as "assistance"—services that have an income value and help families meet ongoing needs, with the exception of work supports for employed families such as childcare and transportation. Conversely, MOE funds are expenditures on benefits and services that the state must make from its own funds as a condition of receiving the TANF grant. Considered "nonassistance," thus not subject to time limits, MOE-funded services could be expanded to include transportation supports such as car purchase and repair subsidies, learning disability testing and remedial GED preparation, physical and mental health support such as counseling and rehabilitative services, and special programs for parents whose children have special needs, elderly caretaker relatives, or recipients with disabilities who do not qualify for disability insurance.

PART 4
Restoring Older Urban Areas

C h a p t e r   1 0

Housing and Urban Communities

Eugenie L. Birch

The housing industry plays an important social and economic role in the United States. Not only do dwellings and their locations denote status in U.S. society, but approximately 4 percent of the nation's Gross Domestic Product is created by residential development. Its effects ripple through the economy. It provides direct employment in construction and related jobs and indirect support for other consumer spending, including home furnishings, appliances, and even garden equipment. The federal government, through surveys conducted by several agencies, among them the U.S. Department of Housing and Urban Development and the U.S. Department of Commerce, keeps close watch on this important industry, monitoring housing starts (usually ranging from 1.2 to 1.8 million units annually), single-family sales, mortgage interest rates, and quality indicators. These statistics provide a picture of the industry, illuminate potential problems, and reveal specific areas for government intervention.

How the Definition of the Housing Problem Has Evolved

The national discourse on shelter issues is more than sixty years old. It includes ownership, quality, and affordability concerns. When housing first became a public policy issue, less than half of the nation's households owned their own homes, one-third lived in substandard conditions, and a substantial number paid a disproportionate amount of their incomes to rent or purchase their dwellings. The housing problem was defined as having multiple dimensions requiring several types of solutions. Important distinctions were made between middle and lower income needs, relating homeownership to the former and housing quality to the latter.

Overall, public policy has sought to encourage and protect capital investment in housing, through a series of ameliorative strategies with two goals: providing a decent home for every American and maintaining the housing supply through construction, reconstruction, or rehabilitation of the nation's dwellings. Policies also linked shelter with the elimination of slums and the physical improvement of city neighborhoods.

In pursuing these goals the United States has had, and continues to have, a very strong private-sector bias, with government intervening only in cases of market failure. However, as definitions of market failure have varied over time, so have the scope and focus of government activities.

Housing Policy: Historical Methods

Understanding today's housing policy requires a review of the older methods of dealing with market failures and the targeted solutions previously employed. Although focusing on a particular issue in American society, their evolution reflects changing concepts of the proper role of government in the life of its citizens. Additionally, some approaches have been more successful than others. Over time, housing policy has moved from adoption of limited, city-based solutions to local problems to more widespread efforts to address national concerns. Policies have employed a battery of tools to deal with the different aspects of the problem, including police power, eminent domain, budgetary resources, plus tax and other financial incentives. Some objectives, such as increasing the rates of middle class ownership and maintaining housing quality, have met with more success than easing housing problems for lower income groups.

Homeownership

Increasing the rates of homeownership has been effective and popular. Centered on using federal influence to improve lending practices and favoring ownership over rental tenure in the federal tax law, these policies have yielded the nation's high number of homeowners.

To improve lending, the federal government created today's modern mortgage system that limits risk for lenders, reduces costs for borrowers, and increases the amount of available capital to finance purchases. During the New Deal, Congress, alarmed by the precipitous decline in housing starts and the dramatic rise in foreclosures, created a multipurpose agency, the Federal Housing Administration (FHA). The FHA developed two programs: It oversaw the development of a massive, self-supporting mortgage insurance program. (This action so increased banks' confidence in their mortgage pools that they lowered consumers' monthly carrying costs and permitted a greater number of households to qualify for mortgages.) It sponsored the creation of a secondary mortgage market, that is, the discounted purchase of bank mortgages. (This activity, by adding liquidity to the financial markets, created more lending capacity in the banking system, thus allowing banks to issue a greater number of mortgages.)

Legislators and FHA administrators were cautious about this new governmental role in housing. Pledging the moral force or reputation of the government but not authorizing actual budget allocations, they insisted that FHA operations be self-financing. This choice significantly influenced FHA practices, especially with regard to what people and properties qualified for insurance. Policies favored the borrowers least likely to default and real estate that would retain value in case of default. Lending formulas determined that white, middle income, nuclear families purchasing new housing located on greenfields or suburbs were "bankable." Minority, low income, and nontraditional households living in central cities were not. The FHA mapped preferred areas, leaving large urban areas ineligible for FHA insurance.

To favor ownership, Congress permitted homeowners to deduct mortgage interest payments and property levies in calculating their income taxes. It also provided for favorable capital gains treatment for home sales, allowing the sellers to plough profits, tax-free, into new units. These policies proved to be powerful incentives to Americans, encouraging them to place their savings in their homes rather than in such alternative investments as bank or stock brokerage accounts.

FHA practices combined with federal tax policies reduced the costs of ownership significantly. They also influenced the type and location of the nation's dwellings and played a role in determining the socioeconomic profile of homeowners. Today, 66 percent of the nation's 98 million households own their own homes. Seventy-five percent of homeowners live in single-family structures. According to the 1997 *American Housing Survey* (AHS), of the nation's 99.4 million units of occupied housing, 51 million are in the suburbs, 34 million are in center cities, and the remainder are in rural areas. Of these, suburbs have a substantially greater number of owned units, 37 million or 73 percent of the stock, while center cities have 17 million owned units or 49 percent of the housing stock. There are also important demographic differences among homeowners. Whites occupy 83 percent of all units and have an ownership rate of 71 percent while only 50 percent of African Americans and 44 percent of Hispanics own. For married couples, the rate is 81 percent; for female-headed households it falls to 52 percent.

Housing Quality and Affordability

The attack on poor housing conditions has taken many forms: adoption of housing code enforcement programs, construction of public housing linked with the elimination of slum dwellings, promotion of rehabilitation through incentives and the creation of income supplements.

In the United States, ensuring minimum standards for dwellings dates from the nineteenth century when municipalities passed building codes aimed at fire prevention and public safety in case of fire. These laws dealt with building materials and construction methods. As time passed, reformers pressed for housing codes that focused on considerations of health and public morality and had strict enforcement programs. The first, New York City's widely emulated Tenement House Act of 1901, mandated basic sanitation (a toilet and running water for each unit), less crowding (no more than one person per room would become a later standard), and light and air (a window in each room, lighted stairwells). For three decades, many cities, especially the larger ones, used housing codes as the primary means of protecting low-income tenants from landlord exploitation. Originally, they applied them only to new construction but gradually extended coverage to all housing.

Housing codes represented a local solution to a local problem. As such, the federal government played no part in promoting housing codes until 1954 when the Housing and Urban Renewal Act mandated code enforcement programs as a precondition for receipt of urban renewal funding.

Today, the federal government still insists on compliance as a condition for new funding arrangements, or for making Section 8 allocations.

Overall, the program has been very successful. By the 1960s, the U.S. Bureau of the Census was able to claim that only 12 to 15 percent of the housing stock was dilapidated or deteriorated. (In fact, while the Census declined to collect statistics about housing conditions after 1960, the U.S. Department of Housing and Urban Development [HUD] continued assessments measuring many features, including the absence of indoor plumbing, central heat, electricity, proper repairs, and sufficient space, in its *American Housing Survey* [*AHS*] begun in 1974.) Today the *AHS* reveals that the majority of the nation lives in dwellings conforming to minimum standards established long ago by the American Public Health Association. Only 1 percent lack indoor plumbing—and some of those are probably vacation cottages—and 8 percent of all housing units were reported to have inadequate heating.

Despite these favorable statistics, low-income households do experience more severe housing problems than the rest of the population. For example, among renting households whose incomes are below the poverty level, 12 percent have some kind of heating problem and 2 percent have plumbing deficiencies. Furthermore, deteriorated housing is usually concentrated in specific neighborhoods. Within older cities, especially those in the Rust Belt where the worst housing is either abandoned or torn down, there are still large areas mixing substandard housing, standard dwellings, and excess vacant land that are usually inhabited by people whom sociologist William Julius Wilson characterizes as the "truly disadvantaged." These neighborhoods represent a major problem whose solution includes housing remediation as one of a battery of ameliorating activities. In addition, some inner-ring or older suburbs face similar risks as new development continues to move to the metropolitan fringe, and some of the new rental housing in outlying areas will go downhill quickly if not maintained.

While some criticize housing codes for raising prices, no one questions that they have successfully raised housing quality in the United States. Local code enforcement remains the principal insurance against new housing deterioration.

During times of crisis, the federal government experimented with delivering public housing, justifying the activity by declaring the need for standard, affordable units. For example, in both World War I and World War II, it built units for defense workers. During the Great Depression, federal public works programs included the construction of low rent housing. The Supreme Court struck down direct construction of public housing by the federal government, but municipalities could still form local housing authorities, which could then receive federal funds..

The Wagner-Steagall Housing Act (1937) adopted this formula in its landmark nonemergency public housing program. Congress authorized the federal government to extend forty-year loans for capital expenses to localities elected to participate.

Overwhelmingly, cities, not suburbs, subscribed to a program that ultimately built about 1.3 million units nationwide. Over the years, the federal government forgave the loans but continued to restrict the authorities' use of the money to construction, not operating costs, maintaining that the rent rolls should cover these latter expenses. Local housing authorities crafted elaborate tenant selection policies to insure balanced budgets. They favored nuclear families with at least one employed wage earner whose salary was in the upper range of low income. While keeping the authorities solvent, these directives disqualified the poorest households.

In the early 1960s, under pressure from many sources, housing authorities modified their tenant selection policies to eliminate income and household composition as admissions criteria. In part, they reacted to critics who insisted that the most needy should qualify for public housing and, in part, to urban renewal leaders who demanded the use of units for relocation programs. Ultimately, Congress passed legislation stipulating that no tenant should pay more than 30 percent of income for rent, regardless of the amount. In many cases, the resulting lowered rents could not cover expenses. Housing authorities met their budgets by deferring maintenance, failing to replace depreciated capital facilities, and reducing services, including security. They lobbied for additional funding, but having scant popular support, they secured only moderate amounts. The outcome was predictable. Neglected and poorly maintained public housing projects became undesirable to all but the most desperate, often dysfunctional households. They experienced high vacancy rates. In fact, by 1992 HUD's National Commission on Severely Distressed Housing reported that 6 percent (or 86,000 units) of the nation's public housing was so blighted that it was unusable.

Today, the nation's public housing stock represents not only some of the nation's worst housing conditions but also serves as evidence of unintended consequences of cumulative policies. Cities originally built large-scale housing projects on multi-acre sites in order to create islands of stable housing within seemingly unending miles of slums, because total eradication of the surroundings was fiscally impossible. This policy, joined with evolving tenant selection and management practices, resulted in the much maligned situation, the concentration or "ghettoization" of the poor.

To remedy this situation, some housing authorities experimented with scattered-site development. Philadelphia, for example, led the nation in this effort, only to regret this decision because its housing authority was unable to maintain these dispersed dwellings efficiently.

In the postwar period, the federal government tinkered with land prices and interest rates to encourage the construction or rehabilitation of low- and moderate-income units, often in large-scale developments. From 1949, with the passage of the Housing and Slum Clearance Act, to 1973 it attempted a variety of approaches. To lower land prices, the government created the urban renewal program, using a formula where the federal budget covered two-thirds of the costs of acquisition, condemnation, and clearance while the localities (states and cities) made up the difference either in cash, in infrastructure investment, or in other equivalent contributions. When this subsidy proved insufficient or inappropriate, Congress included interest-rate subsidy programs (referred to by their section in the legislation, 221(d)3, 235, 236, and 202 programs) to assist privately constructed housing. For example, the 202 program, still in existence, helps finance multifamily rental housing for senior citizens.

The federal government also experimented in the late 1960s and early 1970s with manufactured housing. It hoped to reduce the costs by employing mass-production efficiencies to limit on-site labor. By and large, these programs were not successful, often meeting extreme resistance from labor unions or facing difficulties in adapting to idiosyncratic local building and housing codes. The picture was not entirely bleak. The widely heralded South Bronx settlement on Charlotte Street employed such units (along with a number of other subsidies) to reconstruct an area many had written off as unredeemable. Manufactured housing is only just now coming into general use, mostly for small buildings. The savings are generally in the amount of time needed to put a house or apartment together on site rather than in the cost of construction.

Responding to a variety of complaints regarding the federal approach, President Richard M. Nixon placed a moratorium on all housing and renewal programs in 1973. Besides scapegoating housing and urban renewal efforts as emblematic of "big government," he responded to criticisms that the categorical grant housing program was too time consuming and centralized, too place-restrictive, and subject to corruption and abuse, and that it did not achieve the desired results. Nixon's approach was embodied in the Housing and Community Development Act of 1974. The government abandoned direct, centralized construction methods. It addressed housing with two new measures administered by the Department of Housing and Urban Development. The first, the Community Development Block Grant, allocated monies by formula to localities that determined their use according to their own priorities within loose federal guidelines. The second, Section 8 certificates, are housing vouchers given either to individuals to rent housing on their own or to landlords who made their buildings accessible to low rent tenants. In 1999, HUD's $28 billion budget allocations show that Section 8 certificates and Community Development Block Grants constitute the key elements of contemporary housing policy.

By 1999, the Joint Center for Housing Studies, Harvard University, reported that the federal government currently supported 4.5 million dwellings. Of these, 1.3 million were public housing units, 1.8 million were Section 8 certificates or other subsidies tied to specific buildings, and 1.4 million were free-floating Section 8 units (that is the recipient could use them for any unit anywhere that met federal standards). Together, assisted housing units compose about 4 percent of the nation's stock.

However, this supply is diminishing and will continue to decline in the coming years. Between 1995 and 1998, demolition of substandard public housing and the expiration and nonrenewal of building-based Section 8 certificates has led to the loss of 65,000 units. Furthermore, the federal government anticipates additional decreases as Section 8 agreements on about 14,000 properties—1 million units—will soon come up for renewal. Under today's conditions, customary one-year contract renewals, low caps on acceptable rents, and strict code enforcement programs are disincentives for renewal for landlords of buildings in strong rental markets. The center predicts that forty-four states could lose more than half of their Section 8 subsidized units.

U.S. Housing Today: The Big Problems Are Affordability and Balanced Metropolitan Development

Although national statistics reveal that the partnerships between the federal government and the housing industry have largely overcome two types of shelter problems experienced in the past, low homeownership rates and the high incidence of substandard conditions, housing concerns do persist today. The contemporary definition of the housing problem revolves around affordability. A wide band of the nation's population cannot afford to buy a home. An important subgroup cannot secure shelter by either rental or ownership at the recommended ratios (2.5 times annual income for purchases or 30 percent of income for rental). Solving the affordability problem involves a series of associated concerns: the social, economic, and physical reconstruction of distressed neighborhoods, where 40 percent or more of the population is at the poverty level, the curtailing of wasteful suburban sprawl, and the addressing of the jobs–housing imbalance. These latter issues require coordinated approaches that integrate housing policy with other public and private actions.

While there is no absolute shortage of housing in the United States, there is a lack of affordable units for certain households. Today's median house price is $146,000, and the FHA cap on the value of an insurable home is $208,000. According to the rule of thumb guidelines outlined above, a household should have an income of $58,000 to $60,000 to purchase a house at the median price. However, the national median household income of $37,000 eliminates many. In fact the top price in their range would be $92,500 and there is a limited supply of these units. (Another related theme is that among current homeowners whose median household income is about $40,000 or among the 6.1 million homeowners with incomes below the poverty line, ongoing maintenance of their units may become a serious burden.)

Low-income households naturally experience the greatest problems finding affordable housing. As a group, they have a median household income of $22,000. Not only are they hard-pressed to find a home in their price range (approximately $55,000), but units at their affordable rent,

$550 per month at the median, are becoming scarce. In 1998, HUD reported that 5.3 million (or about 5 percent of the nation's households) very-low-income renters were paying 50 percent or more of their income for shelter. Furthermore, the market is worsening: The number of units renting at below $300 monthly is declining—a 900,000-unit loss occurred between 1996 and 1998 alone—and geographic imbalances are critical; job creation is taking place in suburbs at more than two times the rate in cities. There is no accompanying increase in inexpensive housing in the suburbs leading to a severe jobs–housing mismatch in many areas.

Finally, while the figures are inexact, some 600,000 people are homeless. Their profile reflects low levels of education, few skills, and often difficulties with substance abuse or mental illness; they need not only shelter but also linked services.

Recent Programs for Making Housing More Affordable

Today the nation relies on a series of complex and sophisticated programs to meet housing needs. They tend to leverage the participation of the private sector in increasing the supply of affordable housing, broadening participation among those traditionally excluded from homeownership and addressing issues related to severely distressed public housing and the concentration of poor households in distressed neighborhoods.

The Low Income Housing Tax Credit

In the mid-1980s, the federal government developed a new device, the Low Income Housing Tax Credit (LIHTC), included experimentally in the Tax Reform Act of 1986.[1] Popular among housing providers, Congress renewed the program so that it now has a budgetary authority of about $3 billion annually, sufficient to support 50–60,000 dwelling units per year.

The program is relatively straightforward. The federal government allocates ten-year tax credits to each state according to a formula that allows the equivalent of $1.25 times the number of people in the state. States approve the use of these credits in individual rental projects. Both the acquisition and rehabilitation of existing stock and the construction of new units qualify. Developers can either use the credits against project income or sell them to others, usually corporations, using the proceeds for equity for their projects. These arrangements have proved popular with both for-profit and not-for-profit housing providers.

This law also recognizes the special needs of distressed neighborhoods (called difficult development areas [DDAs]) by increasing the value of the credits by 30 percent when applied in these places. Certified by HUD, a DDA is any census tract where 50 percent of the households have an income of less than 60 percent of the area's median income. The LIHTC program mandates that developers set aside a certain number of dwellings at lower-than-market rents for 30 years. They must allocate either 20 percent of the units to households with 50 percent of the area median income or 40 percent of the units to those having 60 percent of the area median income. It also requires that these tenants pay rents no higher than 30 percent of their income.

Targets for the Secondary Mortgage Market

Establishing secondary mortgage market performance goals for government security enterprises (GSEs) is another important method of increasing the supply of affordable housing. Monitored by HUD, the GSEs (Federal National Mortgage Association [Fannie Mae], the Federal Home Loan Mortgage Corporation [Freddie Mac], the Government National Mortgage Authority [Ginnie Mae]) enjoy certain protections under the law and can borrow money at favorable rates. Although all originally created as government entities, Fannie Mae and Freddie Mac are now privately owned and managed while Ginnie Mae is part of HUD. Their activities are significant. Annually, Fannie Mae expends $1.3 billion and Freddie Mac almost $1 billion. Fannie Mae and Freddie Mac operate without restriction while Ginnie Mae buys only Department of Veterans Affairs and FHA-insured loans. All balance the tension of limiting risks with making profits. In addition, national regulations allow them to bundle (or assemble) and market their holdings as mortgage-backed securities.

Historically, secondary market operations have tended to focus on conservative investments, that is, new construction on greenfields. (In fact, the whole issue of sprawl can be related to the practice of the nation's capital markets. The "Smart Growth" movement is only beginning to call attention to the effects of these decisions.) However, since HUD can set performance goals for the GSEs, it has recently taken a more aggressive, policy-related stance.

At the beginning of the 1990s, HUD set three targets: (1) 40 percent of GSE activities should be dedicated to purchases of mortgages on low and moderate income units, (2) 21 percent of their efforts should be in metropolitan areas where the family median income is less than or equal to 30 percent of the median family income, and (3) 12 percent of their investments should be for affordable housing. To comply, Fannie Mae created a $1 trillion initiative. Aiming to help 10 million families over the next few years, it set up regional offices in twenty-five cities to work with local lending institutions to identify and publicize opportunities.

Leveraging Community Block Grants

With the development of these new tools, many cities have packaged Community Development Block Grants with Low Income Housing Tax Credits, secondary mortgage support, income-enhancing efforts including Section 8 certificates, local real estate tax abatements, and other incentives to support housing development. New York City, which spent more than $50 million in its Mayor's Ten Year Housing Program in the late 1980s and early 1990s, exemplifies these efforts. Nationwide, community development corporations, which have proliferated in the past decade, are direct beneficiaries of this approach. Clearly, housing program administration now demands sophisticated skills in finance.

Improving Public Housing

So many cities have distressed and otherwise unusable public housing units that the federal government devised the HUD-sponsored HOPE VI program. It uses selective demolition and reconstruction to create mixed-income communities on public housing sites. HUD anticipates eliminating 100,000 deteriorated housing units, or about 8 percent of the total public housing units nationally by 2003. It will replace them with 40,000 on-site moderate-income and market-rate dwellings. Plans also call for providing displaced families with Section 8 Certificates to be used off-site. Some cities are employing New Urbanism principles in their designs to give these new low-income neighborhoods a character similar to middle income traditional suburbs.

Between 1993 and 1999 HUD allocated $3.7 billion of HOPE VI

funds to 274 grants. The bulk of the money, $3.5 billion, went to the revitalization of 131 sites. In this effort, many housing authorities are combining HUD funding with other financial instruments. The program has had a slow start-up as local officials have struggled with issues of tenant mix, financing, design, and government approvals. Centennial Place, the former Techwood Homes in Atlanta, and Pleasant View Gardens in Baltimore are examples of successfully completed projects.

The Community Reinvestment Act

The nation has also developed regulatory devices to nudge private sector support for low and moderate income housing, principally, the Community Reinvestment Act (CRA), passed in 1977 and amended in 1989, 1993, and 1999. It requires banks to demonstrate their investment in the communities from which they receive funds. Under this legislation, banks report their mortgage activity, making this information available for public scrutiny. They collect demographic data including race, gender, and income on all mortgage applicants and record their lending processes indicating originations, withdrawals, and denials. Monitored and ranked for their performance, banks seeking to merge or undertake other activities requiring federal permission must show that they have acceptable CRA ratings. Banks have reacted to this law in a number of ways. Some have created internal community development corporations prepared to seek out appropriate opportunities. Others have contributed to intermediary organizations such as New York's Community Preservation Corporation and Philadelphia's Delaware Valley Reinvestment Fund, which manage lending in nontraditional areas. Banks are also regulated by the Financial Institutions Reform, Recovery and Enforcement Act of 1989, legislation designed to prevent the financial crises experienced during the 1980s. Banks must balance their obligations to their depositors while pursing their community responsibilities.

Targeted Federal Housing Programs

While the federal government no longer funds new public housing units for the general population, it does sustain construction programs for special groups. These include the elderly (Section 202), people with AIDS, the homeless, and people who are disabled. However, these are not major programs in terms of amounts of money.

Finally, there are two HUD programs targeting increased homeowner-ship among underrepresented groups, but they are small and experimental. They include the Home Investment Partnership program and Home Ownership Zone designation that allows localities to apply for extra funding assistance in disadvantaged areas.

Housing Policy Planning and Funding

The United States does not have, nor has it ever had, a coordinated, articulated public accounting or evaluation procedure for its housing policy. HUD issues an urban policy report every two years that includes, among other issues, an assessment of housing. Cities receiving HUD funding prepare a Comprehensive Housing Assessment Study annually. (In this report, the locality identifies its housing problems and articulates short- and long-term strategies for their solution, particularly an accounting for expenditures of HUD funds.) Fannie Mae and Freddie Mac, as private corporations, offer annual reports regarding their activities. HUD recently began a database to inventory housing built under the LIHTC program. CRA activities are collected on a bank-by-bank basis.

What Are the Right Policies for the Future?

Today, housing problems revolve around issues of affordability and neighborhood quality in distressed areas. Policy analysts focus attention on the cost of housing, its location, and the inequities in homeownership related to race, gender, and income. In many instances, these problems are found most strongly in inner cities; but many are clearly present throughout metropolitan areas.

Rebuilding disadvantaged communities while addressing related housing problems remains among the most critical national issues. A metropolitan area with a "rotten" core will be weaker than its healthier peers as investors seek alternative locations—leading to a hard-to-arrest decline. In America's 100 largest cities, one in seven census tracts, or 14 percent of their land areas, contain concentrated poverty with all its associated ills. Facing huge gaps in jobs and education as well as in housing, many of these areas also experience severe environmental problems related to brownfields or soil contamination. Currently, several federal agencies are engaged in addressing these urban problems. But they often operate independently. Some examples are: HUD (CDBG, Empowerment and Enterprise Zones,

HOPE VI projects), Environmental Protection Administration (brownfields), Small Business Administration (local commercial activities), Health and Human Services (public assistance, health), Education (schools), and Transportation (TEA-21 programs). Closer coordination, based on strategic planning in which housing policy to provide for mixed income residential areas with rental and ownership opportunities would be one part of a unified approach, is key to reclaiming these areas. The contemporary Smart Growth movement that calls for inner city revitalization along with anti-sprawl measures represents an important beginning and deserves support.

Overall, the public and private sector have developed a diverse set of housing policies based on incentives, regulation, and direct investment. Successful approaches not only produce results but also have political support. Creating new programs is unnecessary but putting more energy into the existing ones is essential.

Recommendations

1. Increase the Low Income Housing Tax Credit.
The LIHTC has been very effective in stimulating dispersed low and moderate-income units. Building on this success, Congress should adjust the ceiling upward, perhaps to $1.75 per person, provide additional incentives for construction in distressed areas, and reduce incentives for greenfields construction.

2. Continue setting income and geographic targets for GSEs.
Setting income and geographic targets for GSEs is resulting in new markets for mortgage lending. Maintaining this pressure is appropriate, especially if coordinated with Smart Growth efforts to slow down sprawl and focus energy on inner city and in-fill suburban opportunities. Working with LIHTC programs should be encouraged.

3. Extend HOPE VI.
HOPE VI, with its emphasis on community building, should be extended to other failed public housing sites. In an associated effort, realistic adjustments to the Section 8 Certificate program would allow for longer contract renewals and some upward movement in rent caps. Some part of the CDBG funding could also be set aside for use in additional HOPE VI efforts.

4. Continue to enforce the Community Reinvestment Act.
CRA enforcement has also expanded financing horizons and should be maintained. Additional support for technical expertise in local communities would allow development of the sophisticated packages now necessary to finance housing.

5. Institute a coordinated and evaluative policy planning system that monitors and adjusts the battery of programs.
Bolstering HUD's urban policy reporting mechanism, officially extending its coverage to metropolitan areas and incorporating all funding agencies would be improvements that would enable pursuit of national goals to address housing and related issues.

NOTE

1. The law actually eliminated some accounting devices favorable to developers of rental housing while substituting the tax credits.

C h a p t e r   1 1

Restoring Natural Resources and Rebuilding Urban Communities

Anne Whiston Spirn

Social, economic, and environmental issues have long been regarded as separate concerns, but they are closely related. Treating them separately leads to unanticipated consequences, costly mistakes, and unrealized opportunities. The neglect of environmental considerations in cities and their separation from issues such as unemployment and community development is one example. Another is the failure to see disinvestment in inner cities, and rural environments and natural resources destroyed by new residential development as part of the same problem, with related social, economic, and environmental repercussions.

Some of the most challenging issues facing the United States today are the result of well-intentioned policies, which had far-reaching, unanticipated consequences besides their desired effect. Federal housing and highway policies are an example. Public funds are squandered when programs are conceived as single-purpose solutions to narrowly defined problems. Such programs often address symptoms rather than causes, and they produce new problems, which may cause social and economic distress and lead to environmental disaster.

The problems facing contemporary cities seem to dwarf the resources available to address them effectively. Social and economic issues, on the one hand, and environmental and aesthetic issues, on the other, compete for attention and scarce funds. Given limited resources, we can no longer afford to address these issues separately. Single-purpose solutions to narrowly defined problems are wasteful of resources and cause unanticipated consequences. We must define multipurpose solutions to comprehensively defined problems. We must seek common solutions to social, economic, and environmental problems.

Buried Floodplains and Vacant Land in Older Urban Neighborhoods

Cities are not separate from the natural world, and they should be developed with an understanding of natural processes, not just social and economic forces. Every region has an underlying landscape structure, which poses constraints and affords opportunities for human settlement. Terrain can be bulldozed and streams diverted at great cost, the natural forces at work can be masked and natural features covered up, but it is much less costly in the long run to work with these forces instead of against them.

In many inner city neighborhoods, vacant land is concentrated in valley bottoms on buried floodplains (Figure 11.1). Water flowing underground, flooding basements and undermining foundations, is a significant cause of abandonment, in addition to political processes like redlining and socioeconomic processes like population migration. That these floodplains were ever developed at all was the result of poor planning and development practices in the nineteenth and early twentieth centuries.

I first became aware of this correlation between buried floodplains and vacant land in 1984, while studying the Dudley Street neighborhood of Boston. I had been told that 30 percent of the land was vacant, and expected to find the vacancy evenly distributed. But when I visited the neighborhood, I discovered that large areas were mostly intact; the hilltops and hillsides had few vacant lots; it was the valley bottoms that were almost completely open. Old maps of the neighborhood showed that a stream had once flowed through the valley, forming the boundary between Dorchester and Roxbury, explaining why a local street was called Brook Street. I traced the successive settlement and abandonment of the neighborhood by

Figure 11.1. Vacant land in the Dudley Street neighborhood was concentrated on buried floodplains in the 1980s. (© Anne Whiston Spirn)

comparing old atlases from 1876 to 1886, 1892, 1903, 1910, 1922, 1934, 1948, 1964, up to the present and found that hill tops and upper slopes had been built on first. Floodplain and stream had been filled in and developed last, and this was where the rental housing had been constructed, with three to six apartments per building. Some of these buildings were abandoned as early as 1910; by 1964 whole areas on the bottomlands were vacant. In the 1970s many buildings owned by absentee landlords burned down, some accidentally, others perhaps deliberately so that owners could collect fire insurance, and by 1985 even more land was vacant. Local people believed the cause was arson; they did not see the probable connection to poor drainage and subsidence on the buried floodplain.

Similar conditions exist in many U.S. cities. The Mill Creek neighborhood in West Philadelphia, where I have worked for the past fourteen years, is a good example. There is a broad, meandering band of land, much of it vacant, where the remaining buildings show signs of subsidence and deterioration. This area winds through the community along the course of an old stream, the original Mill Creek, for which the neighborhood is named. In the late nineteenth century, the stream was put into a sewer, the floodplain was filled in, and buildings were built on top. There is a history of cave-ins of buildings constructed over and adjacent to the sewer, beginning in the 1930s. Following one cave-in in 1961, the city tore down 110 homes.

Public housing projects of the 1950s, 1960s, and 1970s were sometimes built on buried floodplains like those in the Dudley Street and Mill Creek neighborhoods. Mill Creek Public Housing, designed by noted architect Louis I. Kahn, is now in poor condition. Rebuilding houses in these places may simply repeat a cycle of deterioration and destruction when planners ignore the hydrological reasons for building-deterioration and abandonment or when they are overconfident of conventional engineering solutions. Current redevelopment programs, such as the Department of Housing and Urban Development's HOPE VI program, may blindly repeat the mistakes of the past if they merely replace Modernist superblocks, towers, and townhouses in inner city neighborhoods with traditional patterns of grid, house, and porch, without understanding all the underlying causes of abandonment.

In 1985, a local community development corporation in Boston's Dudley Street neighborhood proposed to build dozens of new houses on vacant land, including sites in the bottomland. The story had a happy ending. The architects and planners working on the project were invited to review my students' work, and we had a series of discussions. Ultimately, they adapted a design that one of my students had drawn, which used the low-lying land to create a town common. The new houses are built on higher ground around it (Figure 11.2).

Combined Sewer Overflows Are the Legacy of Bad Development Practices

Burying streams like the brook in Boston's Dudley neighborhood and Philadelphia's Mill Creek, and turning them into pipes that carry stormwater and sewage, created another problem besides subsidence: combined sewer overflows or CSOs. If you drive along the Schuylkill River in Philadelphia after a heavy rainstorm, you may notice that the color of the river turns quite brown and that there is a glaze on the surface, like a lagoon in a sewage treatment plant. After a major rain storm so much stormwater comes off the streets and flows into the sewer—along with all the sanitary sewage from homes and businesses—that there is too much volume for the sewage treatment plant to handle. So some sewage overflows directly into

Figure 11.2. These award-winning new houses for low- to moderate-income families were built on previously vacant land, and a new town common was sited on the bottomland. (© Anne Whiston Spirn)

the river. This is a major problem in Philadelphia and in many other cities like Boston, New York, and Baltimore that were built when it was standard practice for sanitary and storm sewers to be combined.

Federal water quality programs in the 1970s supported the separation of sanitary and storm sewers, and, in many cities, combined sewers were separated, so that stormwater flows straight into rivers without overloading treatment plants. Then scientists discovered that this change did not improve the quality of river water as much as they had expected, because urban stormwater is polluted. It picks up heavy metals and other kinds of dirt and grit from streets. Urban stormwater also contains relatively high counts for fecal bacteria from the feces of all the animals, mainly pets, that live in the cities.

The Environmental Protection Agency is very concerned about the contribution of CSOs and untreated stormwater outfalls to poor water quality in rivers, especially those that are a source of drinking water. The current wisdom is that one should probably treat stormwater runoff as well as sanitary sewage. It becomes an advantage to have a combined system because, if you can manage the treatment, rivers and lakes will be cleaner. The problem, then, is how to deal with massive quantities of sewage that need to be treated right after a rain storm? One solution is to build enormous new sewage treatment plants, and some cities, like Boston, have done that.

Restoring Water Quality and Rebuilding Inner City Neighborhoods

Another way to prevent CSOs would be to detain stormwater on the surface of the ground in order to slow down the time that it takes for stormwater to get into the sewer. The sewage treatment plant would then be able to handle all of the combined sanitary and storm water and there wouldn't be sewage overflows caused by stormwater overloads. A city could build many urban greenways for the cost of a conventional sewage treatment plant and still employ engineers and construction crews, just in a different way. But is such a policy feasible? The Denver Urban Storm Drainage and Flood Control District, created in response to a series of disastrous floods, is a model for how stormwater management might be accomplished in every city.

Natural systems retain stormwater in soil, plants, and streams; rivers overflow onto floodplains, which, if not built upon, protect adjacent areas from flooding. As Denver grew, the ground became covered by more and more buildings and pavement, and it was less able to soak up rainfall, so stormwater flowed more and more rapidly through the watershed into the South Platte River. Buildings and pavement were also built in the floodplains along creeks and rivers. Denver has a semiarid climate, but it sometimes gets torrential rains. In June, when snow is melting in the Rocky Mountains and stream flow is high, such rains can produce devastating floods. In the 1960s, one flood wiped out all the city's bridges and convinced everyone it was time to do something.

Since the 1960s, Denver and surrounding communities have built a network of greenways along the South Platte River and its many tributaries and drainage channels. These are both public open space and part of the region's stormwater and flood control system (Figure 11.3). The stormwater channels look like little streams with berms on either side to keep the water from flooding streets and houses. At Harvard Gulch, for example, the greenway overflows onto a golf course designed to flood if the water rises too high. This system slows down stormwater runoff; instead of

Figure 11.3. Harvard Gulch combines recreation and flood control. It is part of a network of greenways built for storm drainage and flood control along the South Platte River and its many tributaries and drainage channels. (© Anne Whiston Spirn)

reaching the South Platte within a few hours or a day following a rainfall, it takes several days or more to reach the river. By then, floodwaters in the river are receding. The stormwater system is a series of parks that are assets to the neighborhoods around them. The design, maintenance, and construction of these greenways are paid for by the Denver Urban Storm Drainage and Flood Control District, not by a park department budget. Property owners pay a fee based on how much stormwater runoff they contribute to the overall hydrological system. Attending to natural processes in urban planning and design and community development creates opportunities, it is not just a matter of avoiding hazards or problems.

Buried floodplains in urban neighborhoods should be recognized as an important structural part of the landscape, a special zone where new buildings should not be built. An acquisition strategy should address what happens to the buildings that remain in the floodplain. Many of these are plagued with flooded basements, subsidence, and other structural and health issues associated with chronic water problems. Turning these areas into useful open land, whether parks or community gardens, or even parking lots or commercial uses if they are properly designed, would raise the value of the buildings that remain. A landscape infrastructure designed to detain and filter stormwater, thus preventing floods and combined sewer overflows downstream and contributing to improvements in regional water quality, could also improve living conditions in inner city neighborhoods.

I first proposed such an idea in 1985 for Boston, then again in 1988 for Philadelphia's Mill Creek neighborhood as part of the West Philadelphia Landscape Project. Each year since 1996, students in my landscape architecture studio at the University of Pennsylvania have designed wetlands, water gardens, and outdoor classrooms on vacant land in the Mill Creek neighborhood, which would also function as stormwater detention facilities. We have worked with teachers and students at a local middle school to design and implement an urban watershed curriculum. And we have presented these ideas to the Philadelphia Water Department. In 2000, the Philadelphia Water Department submitted a grant proposal to the Commonwealth of Pennsylvania for funds to plan, design, and build a demonstration project on vacant land near Sulzberger Middle School, which will combine a stormwater detention facility to reduce CSOs and an environmental study area for the school. The project will be designed by stormwater engineers, teachers, and students at the middle school, my students, and myself.

Planning, design, and especially the financing of new or reconstructed infrastructure (sewer, water, transportation, power, and communications systems) are among the most effective means of influencing where and how urban growth happens, of protecting and restoring natural resources, and of rebuilding older urban neighborhoods. This work affords great opportunities for education and employment and the creation of new urban amenities, but without managing metropolitan growth, it will not halt or reverse the current migration from older cities to new cities at the edge of metropolitan regions and its social, economic, and environmental consequences.

Inseparable Challenges: Rebuilding Inner City Communities and Reducing Suburban Sprawl

A whole new urban infrastructure is being built on farmlands and forests at the edges of U.S. metropolitan areas: streets, sewers, water and utility lines all facilitated by federal policies and subsidized by public funds. Meanwhile, existing infrastructure in inner city neighborhoods is wasted as homes are abandoned and demolished. Those who protest environmental degradation at the metropolitan edge and those who decry the destruction of inner city neighborhoods share a common cause. Construction of new exurban communities and disinvestment in older cities over the past several decades have destroyed environmental resources at the same time that they have increasingly segregated American society by income and race.

We cannot rebuild inner city communities and sustain the vitality of American cities without addressing the growth of metropolitan regions. We cannot reduce effectively the development pressure at the edge of metropolitan regions, which leads to loss of forest and agricultural land and degradation of streams and rivers, without addressing the decline in urban populations and the quality of urban environments. Only when environmentalists, urbanists, and those concerned about inner cities finally realize that they should work together will we make real progress on both fronts.

There may be a demand for new homes in exurban areas, but is there a need? Consider the familiar scene at the edge of Philadelphia, at the edge of Washington, D.C., Baltimore, Atlanta, Houston, Dallas, Denver, and so many other U.S. cities, of new sewers, streets, and houses being constructed in rural landscapes. While six suburban counties around Philadelphia grew by as much as 12 percent in the 1990s, Philadelphia lost 9 percent of its population during the same period, more than any other U.S. city. Even in metropolitan areas that are growing rapidly, the amount of development taking place at the edge is far greater than is justified by the rate of overall growth. Where are the people going to come from to buy and live in these houses? Since nationally there is no housing shortage, each new house means that an old one is abandoned somewhere else, in slow-growing regions probably in the same metropolitan area.

Some of the richest agricultural soil in the United States now lies, irretrievable, under houses, streets, and parking lots, and many more acres will be built on soon. The area between Los Angeles and San Diego is one of the fastest-growing districts in the country. Agricultural land in Orange County, California, is now used for strawberry fields, as a holding pattern prior to development (Figure 11.4). The strawberry plants cover the land and the harvest provides income to help defray the property taxes in this rapidly developing area. Much of what is being built today in Orange County is mixed use at high densities. This type of development presum-

Figure 11.4. These agricultural fields in Orange County, California, are a temporary land use. (© Anne Whiston Spirn)

ably pleases the new urbanists, who say that we ought to build places that are denser and use less land, thereby conserving energy. But the real issues are how much needs to be built and what is being done both to the country's natural resources and to existing cities by continuing to build on farms, forests, grasslands, and deserts in exurban areas?

Inner city neighborhoods of Detroit, built in the age of the automobile, always looked suburban because they were composed of free-standing homes laid out in a dispersed settlement pattern. Drive through these neighborhoods today, and you feel like you are out in the countryside: So many houses have been abandoned and demolished that those remaining are separated by open fields. But there are still sewers under the streets, there are water lines, gas lines, and electrical lines, there is a whole infrastructure in these neighborhoods, built to support a much larger population. Profits were made, developers moved on, neighborhoods have been abandoned, but the infrastructure is still there. Infrastructure lies fallow in many other cities across the country. Yet new streets, sewers, water, and power lines are being put in place, laboriously and expensively, with public subsidy, to support development on agricultural land at the edges of metropolitan areas.

What happens to the people who remain behind in existing urban neighborhoods? In 1997, the *Philadelphia Inquirer* published a story about the Rhawnhurst neighborhood in Northeast Philadelphia, which was built primarily since the 1950s. It is made up of relatively modest, suburban-style homes and rowhouses. The houses are in good condition; trees and shrubs have matured; it is a pleasant place, its population ethnically and racially diverse. Astonishingly, 68 percent of the homeowners are over 55, although this is a lower proportion than other neighborhoods in a city where 52 percent of the houses are owned by people over the age of 60. Homeowners interviewed about their plans for the future were very concerned about whether or not they will be able to sell their homes when they want to move or can no longer live on their own. In ten or fifteen years, when they put their houses on the market, what will happen? Will these perfectly sound houses go the way of earlier abandoned properties in older neighborhoods?

In addition to the social costs, think about the natural resources wasted when solid houses are abandoned and destroyed. Consider what it takes to build a new house: the trees for the lumber, the metal for nails, pipes, and so on, plus the energy it takes to manufacture and transport the building materials. Avoiding unnecessary building is another aspect of energy conservation and natural resource protection.

We should eliminate public policies that subsidize the construction and ownership of new homes in new communities when we have so many homes that are already built. Federal policies should not continue to subsidize the construction of new sewers, streets, and water and power lines in exurban areas when we have so much infrastructure already built, now underutilized because so many people have moved out of existing cities. Federal subsidies for new residential construction were introduced in the 1930s to create jobs and get people back to work, for the building trades represented a large proportion of the unemployed during the Depression. Subsidies were expanded after World War II, augmented by the federal highway program and mortgages for veterans that favored the purchase of new homes rather than older ones. These programs had many benefits, but they also had devastating, unforeseen social, economic, and environmental consequences. Together with private investment, such as large-scale residential development, and banking practices, such as redlining, they reshaped the American rural and urban landscape, destroying farmland, forests, and urban communities. New public policy could reverse these effects and reshape the landscape once again.

Recommendations

1. In rebuilding urban communities, seek common solutions to social, economic, and environmental problems.

In coming years, cities will spend billions of dollars to reduce combined sewer overflows, which are caused by stormwater overloading the system. Paying for corrective measures is necessary to meet water-quality standards for rivers, lakes, and harbors. This expenditure could also be an extraordinary opportunity to make major improvements in older urban neighborhoods—if policymakers can look beyond traditional engineering solutions.

2. Stop subsidizing exurban growth.

The U.S. government should stop all federal subsidies, direct and indirect, for the construction of new urban infrastructure and new homes outside existing urban areas. This policy would be analogous to those of the several states that have growth management or Smart Growth legislation (see Chapter 3) If there is demand for exurban development, let the market bear the full cost.

Chapter 1 2

Downtowns: Competitive for a New Century

Paul R. Levy

This photograph of Market Street looking west toward City Hall in downtown Philadelphia was taken in February 1948 (Figure 12.1). It is not holiday shopping season; it is not rush hour; it is a scene typical of American cities prior to suburbanization. Here is my goal in life: to restore this level of pedestrian activity downtown. Despite all the positive work done in the past forty years in downtown renewal, Philadelphia has a long way to go to bring back this volume of workers, residents, shoppers, and visitors to downtown streets.

The Decline of Philadelphia's Economy and the Renewal of Center City

To understand the challenges that confront Philadelphia today, it is important to understand the factors that caused its decline and which are spurring its current revival.

At the time of the Declaration of Independence, Philadelphia was the largest city in North America with 24,000 residents, and Independence Hall was at the city's western boundary. The town continued to grow to the west and by the early 1800s, most of the area planned by William Penn

Figure 12.1. Downtown Philadelphia on an ordinary February day in 1948, before suburban development was a strong competitor to downtown. (Photo courtesy of Center City Philadelphia.)

had been settled. When industrialization began, it occurred on open land north, south, and west of the original colonial city.

The city went through a very rapid process of industrialization, beginning in the 1820s and 1830s. Philadelphia did not evolve as a one industry town like Pittsburgh, Detroit, or Dayton, but as a highly diverse economy that included a very large garment and textile industry, producing men's and women's clothing and Stetson hats. Philadelphia also manufactured precision machine tools, saws, and the Baldwin Locomotive. The city specialized in sugar refining and, later, oil refining.

The typical industrial neighborhood had a factory surrounded by row houses within walking distance for the workers. As manufacturing has become less labor intensive, more mechanized, and more computerized, and as industry moved first to the suburbs, then to the south and west, then overseas, Philadelphia went from having over half of its workforce in manufacturing down to about 12 percent. Today, whole sections of the city are left with only the remnants of the industrial age. Once there were seventy-eight breweries, a major source of employment. Now there are none, although the relics of the buildings are still here.

In the neighborhoods where the factories have departed, much of the population has gone as well, leaving deteriorated or abandoned houses and acres of vacant land. A typical Philadelphia row house that might sell downtown in Society Hill for $500,000 can be bought in many of these areas for as little as $1,000. While Philadelphia still has many stable working class communities, devastation and abandonment define much of the older industrial city, and residents here are far removed from job opportunities.

To address these problems, Philadelphia, like most other cities, has benefited from federally funded housing redevelopment programs in low- and moderate-income neighborhoods since the 1960s. For over thirty years, the city has been renovating existing housing and commercial areas and building new housing with parking or garages. But population and job loss have continued nonetheless.

Starting in the 1950s and 1960s, the federal government also made a tremendous amount of money available for downtown renewal and it is on this process that I will focus. Cities were near the top of the national agenda for about a decade in this country. Planners, like Philadelphia's Edmund Bacon, had the benefit of major federal dollars to carry out a program of comprehensive renewal for downtown, essentially the area originally planned by William Penn between the Delaware and Schuylkill Rivers. Through comprehensive public–private efforts at acquisition, demolition, rehabilitation, and new construction, this area has successfully made the transition to the post-industrial economy of the late twentieth century.

How Downtown Philadelphia Was Transformed

As the city's manufacturing base went into decline, the port along the Delaware River ceased to function as a place that imported raw materials and exported finished goods. Simultaneously, the containerization of cargo rendered obsolete many older piers that had relied on manual labor. Part of the renewal work of the 1960s was the relocation of the remaining working piers to new container facilities to the north and south and the reclamation of the downtown waterfront for public use and entertainment. Renamed Penn's Landing, the central waterfront has emerged as a place for major festivals, and adjacent piers have been converted to housing, clubs, and other entertainment uses. Now there is a proposal to build a regional scale shopping and entertainment center on the waterfront.

Moving west from the Delaware waterfront is the area known as Society Hill. While other cities were demolishing their past, Philadelphia was a national leader in reclaiming this area through historic preservation. As the port had declined, so had the economic base of adjacent communities, leaving deteriorated housing and obsolete structures. Hundreds of dilapidated historic townhouses were restored and sold as middle class housing. Older warehouses were demolished and new construction included townhouses, condominiums, and three apartment towers that are a landmark in the area.

Society Hill was a hugely successful turnaround, spurring a 20 percent increase in the population downtown at the same time that the city overall was losing 30 percent of its residents. Today, Philadelphia has the third largest downtown residential population in the United States, and the median household income in downtown Philadelphia is equal to that of the region's most affluent suburbs.

To the north of Society Hill, Independence National Historic Park was created by preserving many of the eighteenth century buildings that served as the birthplace for American democracy. The area was generously landscaped and staffed with park rangers to create an attractive tourist destination. At the same time, to create a version of the Washington mall, there was wholesale demolition of numerous nineteenth century loft buildings of the type we would be inclined to save today. Currently the city has sponsored a redesign of the mall, adding back buildings and making other efforts to break down the barriers created by the 1960s monumental modernist architecture that surrounds the mall.

Along East Market Street, Philadelphia once had seven department stores. But, from 1955 to 1977, 15,000 regional shopping centers were built in suburbs across the country, and the Philadelphia region built its share. As a result, by the 1970s, all but two of Market Street's department stores had closed. This trend was finally reversed when the Rouse Company opened the country's first downtown regional shopping center, the Gallery at Market East, in 1977. The center was doubled in size in 1982 with direct connections to the regional rail lines. The historic Lit's Department Store was renovated as well, as back-office space for a major bank.

In 1950, looking west from City Hall, you would have seen what was called the Chinese Wall, a vast elevated railway extending all the way to 30th Street Station. Shortly after, the railway viaduct and related industrial warehouses were demolished, using urban renewal dollars and clearing the way for a new office district, called Penn Center. Later the city's two commuter rail lines were connected underground, effectively linking the new office district with the region's workforce. Today, over 60 percent of downtown workers use mass transit to get to work.

By the 1970s a whole new office district began to emerge and the volume of office development accelerated in the 1980s. Throughout his tenure as head of the City Planning Commission, Edmund Bacon had been able to enforce an informal agreement that no new tower would be taller than the statue of William Penn atop City Hall. But there was no legal height limit, and Liberty Place inaugurated the transformation of the skyline. By 1990, a whole new generation of office buildings towered above William Penn's hat, as downtown emerged as a post-industrial center for finance, insurance, real estate, law, architecture, and engineering firms.

Putting Downtown Renewal in Perspective

The achievements of downtown renewal should be placed in perspective. Even as a remarkable transformation occurred, suburbanization continued. There are now eighteen regional malls in the Philadelphia metropolitan area, including the huge concentration of shopping at King of Prussia. Shopping in the city center is only a small fraction of all retail activity in the region.

There are also many of what Joel Garreau termed edge cities along Route 202, Interstate 76, and the Pennsylvania Turnpike and in the New Jersey suburbs. During the 1980s, all the region's employment growth took place in such areas while the city was steadily losing jobs. Even as Philadelphia added a lot of office space downtown in the 1980s, the Pennsylvania and New Jersey suburbs were adding buildings at a faster rate. Work within the region has become decentralized. We now have more people commuting from homes in the suburbs to work in the suburbs, than making the traditional commute into the city.

Philadelphia today is thus a city of enormous contrasts. The restored downtown is an office center, a retail and residential center, a center for arts and entertainment, and increasingly a destination for tourists. Yet the older, industrial city is very thinned out and steadily losing population. The issues in these areas are ones of crime, safety, housing deterioration, underperforming schools, and the residents' lack of preparedness to access the new jobs in the region.

Repositioning Downtown for the Twenty-first Century

As downtowns have become the most important economic generators for older communities, cities need to position them to compete more effectively with the suburbs and to play a larger role in the metropolitan economy. The current trend for downtowns is to move beyond being simply places for work and shopping to consolidate their position as the regional center for arts, culture, entertainment, fine dining, and increasingly, for sports.

In Philadelphia, Broad Street south of City Hall had been the office district for the first half of the century with a lot of wonderful old buildings, as well as the Academy of Music and the University of the Arts. Plans to remake the area as an arts and entertainment district had been formulated in the 1980s, largely through funding from local foundations. But when Mayor Rendell took office in 1992, he seized upon the idea to reposition this area as an Avenue of the Arts, aggressively seeking state funding and private contributions to implement the plans.

Streetscape improvements were installed. The Merriam Theater was renovated, a new theater, the Wilma, was built in conjunction with a parking garage, and renovations commenced at the Academy of Music. Other new facilities include a jazz performing hall, small theaters, and an expanded high school for the creative and performing arts. The capstone of this project, a new regional performing arts center, will open in 2002. The Philadelphia Orchestra will move there, freeing the Academy of Music for other performances. To reinforce these efforts, Mayor Rendell's administration placed a major emphasis on the entertainment aspects of downtown with numerous festivals and special events. The net result is a significant increase in restaurants and nightlife, the re-tenanting of older office buildings, and the conversion of others to apartments and student housing.

The other major trend affecting most downtowns has been the growing importance of the hospitality industry. More than 200 American cities have built major centers in their downtowns to attract conventions and trade shows. Philadelphia's new center, completed in 1993, has been highly successful, not only in drawing people into the downtown, but in creating new economic activities, particularly on the east side of Center City. This area had steadily weakened as office tenants had migrated west. But, by the end of the 1990s, close to 3,000 hotels were under construction, largely through renovations of older buildings east of City Hall, including the historic PSFS office tower. Nationally known, visitor-oriented entertainment, retail, and restaurant establishments were also locating in close proximity to the Convention Center.

Philadelphia no longer exports manufactured products, but it has begun to redefine itself as a place that imports people and finds entertaining ways for them to leave their money behind. Building on the success of the Convention Center, the city has begun to market itself aggressively as a tourism destination. This too has helped support the restaurant renaissance downtown.

Even so, the hospitality industry, by the most generous definition, employs only 20 percent of the downtown workforce in hotels, in arts and entertainment facilities, and in the retail sector. The jobs that are being created, however, are important replacements for the unskilled and semi-skilled jobs lost in the manufacturing sector. The average wage in a hotel, before tips, is $19,000 a year; Philadelphia residents hold 80 percent of these jobs. By contrast, the average wage in an office building, where 60 percent of Center City's jobs are located, is $56,000 a year. But Philadelphia residents hold only 40 percent of these jobs.

One of the major challenges facing the city is retaining and attracting not only entry-level jobs, but also high-skilled, high-wage jobs in the office sector. A vital downtown not only imports people, it must be able to export services to an increasingly international economy. An increase in workers can also translate into an increased demand for downtown housing.

Bringing the Private Sector into Managing Downtown

The organization I direct, the Center City District (CCD), is what is generally called a business improvement district (BID). Organizations like the CCD began in the United States in the 1980s, driven by two factors. First, as the federal government decreased its support for urban areas, cities began to cut back on services. Second, when elected officials had to make tough decisions for allocating scarce resources, they faced a clear-cut choice. Downtown Philadelphia may have 40 percent of the jobs in the entire city, but it houses only 5 percent of the electorate. So a mayor or city councilperson who wants to be reelected has to focus on the needs of the 95 percent of the voters who don't live downtown. If you are allocating scarce resources as an elected official, it is totally appropriate that you focus on the neighborhoods where the people who vote live. Downtowns thus faced a double hit in the 1980s: a reduction in federal resources coming into cities plus local allocation decisions that favored the neighborhoods.

At the same time downtowns had to compete with well-managed suburban office campuses and regional shopping centers. Shopping center tenants typically pay a "common area maintenance" charge over and above their rent to maintain the public areas, the wonderful trees and fountains that you see in shopping centers today, the entertainment, the advertising budgets, the upkeep of the free parking lots. Similarly, Disneyland or any other theme park or entertainment destination is clean and well maintained because there is a dedicated revenue stream to do it. That is not to say that we should turn cities into Disneylands. But to be competitive in a world where highly mobile businesses, visitors, and residents have a wide range of well-managed choices, downtowns need the same management tools as a regional shopping center, an office campus, or a theme park. Quite simply, as municipal resources have declined, the standards and expectations for the public environment have risen.

By 1990, the deterioration in municipal services had left Philadelphia's downtown filthy. It was perceived as unsafe and unattractive, a place that people should avoid. Indeed, like many cities, we suffered from the phenomenon I call pride of avoidance. What's pride of avoidance? It is when two suburban residents meet and one says, "I haven't been downtown in ten years." And the other retorts, "Well that's nothing. I haven't been downtown in twenty years!" Our goal of course is to foster a pride of attraction. "Have you been downtown lately? Have you seen what opened there?" But in the absence of a business improvement district, Philadelphia's 2,100 downtown property owners had no legal mechanism to act in concert to address these challenges.

Nonetheless, Philadelphia's Center City began the decade with extraordinary assets, the results of thirty years of public and private planning and investment: 38 million square feet of office space, 2,400 retail establishments, 300,000 downtown workers, and 75,000 middle and upper income residents living in all types of housing. The new convention center, which was planned in the 1980s and opened in 1993, was very much a driving force in helping to create the BID. We asked, "When the Center opens, will Philadelphia be ready for this business? Will new visitors coming downtown feel safe, comfortable and encouraged to return?"

To create a BID, property owners vote a supplementary assessment—over and above what they pay to the city—to fund dedicated services within the boundaries of their district. In our case, it is a 5 percent surcharge on top of the real estate property tax, with payment going directly to our organization. We are a private-sector organization with the authority to assess property owners in the same way that the city does. Once a majority of the owners vote to create the district the extra assessment becomes a mandatory charge. It is the equivalent of the common area maintenance charge in the shopping center.

When our operations began in 1991, we focused on just two things: cleanliness and safety. We defined what we did as supplementing, but not replacing, city services. Municipal employees clean the streets and empty trashcans; our private-sector workers clean each sidewalk from curb line to building line three times a day. We manually and mechanically sweep them; the dirtier sidewalks are cleaned seven times a day. We do graffiti removal, and we track the results. We have seventy people working seven days a week just on basic maintenance in the downtown.

Secondly, we deploy another group of forty uniformed, unarmed individuals we call community service representatives (CSRs) (Figure 12.2). They are equipped with two-way radios and patrol on foot throughout downtown. Their radios connect back in to our offices where, by agree-

Figure 12.2. One of the community service representatives who work for the Center City Philadelphia business improvement district. (Photo courtesy of Center City Philadelphia.)

ment with the city, all the police who patrol on foot and on bikes share the facility with our CSRs. Police and civilians share locker rooms, jointly stand roll call each morning, and jointly plan daily deployment strategies. Our CSR have no arrest powers and carry no weapons, but they serve as the "eyes and ears" for the police.

Back in 1992, we linked together by modem the two police districts in the downtown that overlapped our business improvement district and began computerized crime tracking. Ever since, we have been producing color-coded intensity maps to show concentrated areas of crime. We can map types of crime by time of day, which then allows the police to make intelligent deployment decisions. The combined effect of additional deployment and computerization has been very significant: a 38 percent decrease in serious crime within our district, with no displacement of these crimes outside the district.

We frequently conduct customer satisfaction surveys, and these show that people believe that downtown has become much safer. This is almost more important than the real numbers. We have increased the sense of public safety and changed the image of downtown. Things are still not perfect by any means, but the trend lines are going in the right direction.

All our people on the street are also trained to function like a walking hotel concierge. They give directions to orient people, and we have kiosks where we provide information about arts, culture, and retail within downtown. We do the types of things that police officers don't have time to do, like take photographs of visitors or escort them to locations. All our CSR are also trained in first aid and CPR. We learned early on that visibility is key, that doing the job is important, but so is being seen doing the job. So we took a lot of care in designing our uniforms.

People often argue that there is an anti-tax environment in this country. But we now have over 1,200 BIDs in North America. What I think is actually happening is a revolt against poor service. People will pay for services that they can see and touch. So a highly visible uniformed presence and a focus on customer service are key to everything we do.

Making Downtown More Competitive

After we had achieved basic cleanliness and improved on safety, we began to work with retailers on an effort to promote evening shopping. We borrowed techniques from the suburban shopping centers by producing

Figure 12.3. Putting entertainment on the street to animate the public environment. Pictured is a bed-making contest for hotel managers—anything to draw a crowd, and the television cameras. (Photo courtesy of Center City Philadelphia.)

advertisements for radio, print, and ad cards on rail lines. We put entertainment on the street with the goal of animating the public environment; we do events for families and children, blow up balloons, stage bed-making contests for hotel managers, anything to draw a crowd—and the television cameras (Figure 12.3).

Studies by the Annenberg School for Communication show that people's fear of crime relates more to watching the evening news than to the actual amount of crime in their neighborhood. Television is a very powerful medium. Local news often focuses first on the fires, the disasters, the murders, as if that were all that was going on, creating incredibly negative images of cities. The media wants good visuals and, unfortunately, a train wreck is a compelling image. So, we are in the business of focusing attention on the positive images that convey the good things that are happening downtown.

Our evening promotions, done in partnership with the city, were enormously successful. We then branched out with advertising aimed at the regional resident, focusing on arts and entertainment and restaurants, which we knew from market research could draw suburbanites into the city. Within the past two years we added a little edge and humor to our ads, contrasting the boredom of suburbia with the excitement of Center City. We could have never done this eight or nine years ago. Today, we have a strong enough base that we can afford to take this risk.

It is not all image making. We have also confronted the truly difficult issues within the downtown. At the beginning of the decade, we had a population of at least 500 individuals who routinely were living and begging on the streets of Center City. We began first by working with local government to improve the management and delivery of services for drug and alcohol recovery, mental health, and job training. We funded our own outreach teams that work with people on the street to connect them with services.

Many of our maintenance initiatives create semiskilled and unskilled jobs. So, we have partnered with social service and job training programs to hire their graduates who are in recovery or making the transition from welfare to work. We are not a social service agency, but an employer. There are no separate rules for the disadvantaged people we hire. They have to show up and work. But we have been able to create hundreds of opportunities both within the downtown and in service contracts we have entered into for maintaining the landscaping on the Vine Street Expressway, plus contracts for sidewalk cleaning, graffiti removal, and landscape maintenance in three adjacent residential neighborhoods and two other business improvement districts. All the individuals who work on these contracts are formerly homeless individuals or individuals making the transition from welfare to work. They start out making $6.50 an hour plus benefits and can move up to more responsible jobs paying $9 and $10 an hour within our organization. We help get disadvantaged workers started on the employment ladder.

With substantially improved city services and increases in transitional and permanent housing for the formerly homeless, there are only about 100 individuals who remain today on the streets of our downtown.

Financing Permanent Improvements

Our district started out with a five-year life. In 1994 we went back to the property owners and won reauthorization for twenty years. This longer commitment allowed us to borrow money, secured by our annual revenues, in order to make capital improvements.

We began with an analysis of where sidewalks were in good condition and where they were terrible. We sold $21 million worth of tax-exempt bonds backed only by district revenues and carried out a comprehensive streetscape improvement program: installing new corners with accessible ramps and planting over 400 trees. With the cooperation of the city and with $5 million they contributed, we took down all the tall light poles designed only to light roadways in the retail district and replaced them with 16-foot-tall light fixtures that doubled and tripled the level of illumination on the sidewalks. If the most dramatic thing we have done in ten years is eliminating litter, new lighting is close behind.

For visitors, we have developed a comprehensive, new graphics system, installing color-coded maps midblock on every block, showing where you are and what is within a ten-minute walk. North is not always at the top of the map, whatever direction you are facing is at the top. You no longer have to turn your body or the map upside down to orient yourself. Every corner has directories of nearby attractions. We are trying to make the city center legible and friendly to tourists and people from the suburbs who haven't been downtown in a long time.

Back in 1996, we started to look at older office buildings with low occupancy rates to see how they could be converted to apartments. We had a design and development team look at how to simplify codes, did the analysis to demonstrate that attracting residents is economic development, and then lobbied successfully for a ten-year tax abatement for conversion of vacant buildings to residential use.

We also publish and distribute brochures promoting downtown as a place to live. We set a goal of adding 2,000 new residents by the year 2000 and 10,000 new residents by 2010 and have been advocating a package of policy changes to make this goal more achievable. So far, over 1,200 units of housing have been developed as a result of the abatement incentive.

Our most recent work has focused back on the office sector. We have lunchtime concerts in front of office buildings. We are setting up shop within office lobbies during lunch hours, bringing the police and community service representatives to respond personally to public safety concerns. We work with building managers to address the concerns of tenants. We give away coupons encouraging people to take advantage of downtown retail, arts, and culture. This is all part of an effort to enhance downtown as a place to work and to retain employees by conveying the exciting opportunities that are here.

The overall trends for us have been very strong. Office occupancy has been steadily climbing. There has been a slight downturn in retail occupancy, but this is largely because Chestnut Street is being reconstructed and many buildings are in transition. The Convention Center has performed extraordinarily well, bringing 1.4 million people per year into the downtown, which has driven an increase in both hotel occupancy and room rates. After losing jobs within the downtown for many years, we have finally started a rebound.

Increasingly, our organization has been focusing strategically, doing research and analysis on employment trends and sectors of growth. We have three times the national average of engineers, seven times the number of lawyers, but are really lagging in information technology firms. This gives us a clear indication that we should be putting our energy into supporting efforts to continue to lower local tax and regulatory burdens to insure that we are a competitive location for the twenty-first century. But our goal can be stated more simply: to increase the number of people on the street—workers, residents, shoppers, tourists, conventioneers, and people drawn for entertainment—to recreate 1948.

Lessons for Public Policy

What can mayors do to get cities out of their current difficulties; what kind of help should we expect from the state and federal governments?

During the era of the New Deal in the 1930s, 50 percent of the American people lived in large central cities. Today, it is about 24 percent The majority of Americans live in the suburbs, which means that a majority of elected officials in Washington represent the suburbs. In the words of Neil Pierce, this is the post-Federal era for American cities. As is typical for older cities, there is little systematic regional governance in the Philadelphia metropolitan area. So Philadelphia has to rely more on its own revenue and initiatives to deal with the problems created by the loss of jobs and residents to the suburbs: 23 percent of the people living in poverty, the deterioration of the housing stock, the problems of the schools.

Paris gets 60 percent of its operating budget from the French government. The city of Philadelphia gets only 16 percent percent of its operating budget from the American government. Given current political realities, if cities are going to receive any new outside funds they are likely to come from their states, from private foundations, or from improvement districts like ours.

Recommendations

1. Make city government more efficient.
A lot of cities have attempted to raise revenue by raising taxes to compensate for a shrinking tax base. All they succeed in doing is driving out businesses and the middle class. The only way you can maintain or reduce current levels of taxation without cutting services is to lower the cost of government. So, most cities are looking creatively at downsizing. How do you continue to deliver services effectively and in a consolidated fashion but lower the cost? The reality for a city like Philadelphia was that our population was declining by 30 percent, but the number of municipal employees was growing by 30 percent.

Mayors can do many things to improve competitiveness and efficiency, often the same things that business would do: focus on the customer, computerize, create internal incentives for efficiency and productivity. This doesn't mean giving up the commitment to social services and low income programs. It means running them well and running them in a more cost-effective fashion.

2. Make city administration friendly to investment.
Cities need to do more to encourage the people who do want to invest. If you were attempting to build housing in most surrounding suburbs, the permitting and political battles are enormous up front. However, once the permitting process takes place, it is relatively easy to develop. Whereas, within the city, you have five-six-seven different agencies who must give approval. If you want simply to put an awning on a historic property on Walnut Street in downtown Philadelphia, you need six separate agencies to approve it. If agencies one through four approve it, and agency five turns you down, there is no consolidated permitting process. You have to start over. So there are lot of things that mayors can do to improve the investment climate for business, not by eliminating regulations that insure public safety, but through regulatory simplification.

3. Build on the city's competitive advantages.

Mayors can also help focus attention on the competitive advantages of cities. Michael Porter at Harvard has been looking at the inner city and low income areas, not as social service and welfare problems, but as places to restart the private market. What are the competitive advantages for business in locating in inner cities? We know, for example, that office buildings and retail stores need plate glass. So glass suppliers often locate near downtown. We know that law firms need printers, so downtown law firms can support a cluster of inner city printers. We need to examine how the post-industrial economy of the downtown can connect to and generate new production and distribution jobs in the inner city. Food distribution, for example, can be a very big business for cities that are expanding restaurant and entertainment destinations.

Thinking about how to make cities more competitive should be a number one goal for mayors. The mayor of Milwaukee, John Norquist, has a great title for the first chapter in his new book, *The Wealth of Cities:* "You Can't Build a City on Pity." It is a critique of the mayors who have been crying poverty. "We are desperate, helpless, so please come save us." But there is no longer a federal doctor coming to save American cities.

4. Create business improvement districts.

An improvement district like ours can create funds for better maintenance and public safety and can also fund long-term improvements.

5. State and federal programs should reward cities that do things well.

What I would be looking for from governors and from the national government is relatively modest, but essential. The federal government and the states ought to be looking for how to reward American cities that are attaining fiscal stability and improving the efficiency of local government. Aid should not just follow a per capita funding formula, which has the effect of rewarding increased poverty and deterioration, but should provide increased resources to reward cities whose social service programs are well managed. This is the number one issue, because clearly the major burden that cities carry is the burden of poverty.

6. Find regional solutions.

I also think governors and the federal government ought to be creating incentives for regional solutions. It is not likely in the Philadelphia area that cities and suburbs will voluntarily embrace and draw an urban growth boundary to direct growth. But what are the incentives that higher levels of government can offer for smarter growth policies? Despite the different government jurisdictions and the complexities of regional politics, city and suburbs all belong to the same economic region, and our futures are bound together. In the new century, it is regions that will compete, or fail to compete, internationally; and it is the downtown that can be the heart and a vibrant, twenty-four-hour hub of the region.

Afterword: The University and Civic Engagement

Judith Rodin
President of The University of Pennsylvania

The essays you have just read reflect three important facts that may be immediately evident only to those who are close to their source. First, they reflect the continuation into a new century of the long and distinguished tradition of urban planning and public policy research at the University of Pennsylvania. Second, they reflect the central role of "The Urban Initiative"—one of Penn's six strategic academic priorities—in the University's Agenda for Excellence, our vision of what it means to be a leading international research university in the twenty-first century. Indeed, this book grew out of an interdisciplinary seminar that is a central part of The Urban Initiative at the University of Pennsylvania. Finally, these essays reflect Penn's institutional commitment not only to understanding urban and related social issues through the University's traditional missions of research and education but also to engaging comprehensively and practically those issues and problems, as they affect our city, our region, and, most important, our own West Philadelphia community.

We believe that it is not enough for universities to attract as teachers and produce as graduates brilliant and imaginative doctors, lawyers, scholars, and scientists who will push the envelopes of their disciplines or professions, if we do not also engage them in the larger issues of our day, in the ferment of our times, our society, and our cities.

We believe that colleges, universities, museums, libraries, historical societies, and other cultural institutions have a central role to play in conceiving and implementing an urban agenda for our twenty-first-century communities. Increasingly, these institutions are emerging as the venues around which strong, inclusive, well-functioning modern communities can form. They are, in fact, the new loci of America's "civil society."

We believe that universities in particular can be the exemplars of a new kind of civic engagement, neither easy nor accidental, but strategic, comprehensive, intense, and purposeful. At its best, this new kind of civic engagement weaves itself in and through every aspect of campus life, from medical research and particle physics to classical studies, student volunteerism, and economic development.

Because the culture of higher education is notoriously resistant to change, this new kind of civic engagement must become not a *second* thought or an *after*thought but a self-conscious and permanent part of the ethos and mission of American higher education in the twenty-first century. At Penn and other civically engaged universities around the country, the elements of this new and comprehensive vision of our institutions' civic roles are taking shape.

More than at any time in the past, universities play an essential role in sorting out what we know and what we do not know, so that political leaders, journalists, and ordinary citizens can make sense of the huge amounts of data available today. Universities and their faculties routinely interpret and publicize the results of their research for the general public. By providing clear information, we help to frame and inform important public policy debates and explode negative popular myths that breed unfounded cynicism.

Academically based service-learning courses find synergy in the combination of scholarship and service, in their discovery of theory through practice as much as through the application of academic knowledge to the real problems of real communities. This interaction, this *unity*, of theory and practice is a part of Penn's "genetic material" from our founder, the great statesman and scientist Benjamin Franklin. In a typical Penn program, for example, a student performs service as part of an internship that is coordinated with scholarly research, to the mutual benefit of education, research, and service.

Universities, as citizens themselves, increasingly shoulder an extensive and growing range of civic responsibilities for the quality of life in their neighboring communities—for elementary and secondary education, employment opportunities, economic development, security and policing, sanitation, transportation, local business development, real estate management, cultural life, retail and shopping services—and the manner in which they do so is an important example to their students and to other institutions. At Penn, we require that all of our University construction projects create substantial access for women and minorities, and we are investing in small businesses that create opportunities for welfare-to-work recipients and other members of our local community. Indeed, our Wharton entrepreneurship program is helping to develop the small businesses' plans. Through these and other similar efforts, we are working to build community capacity and infrastructure, and we have become a forceful catalyst for change.

In Philadelphia, Boston, and other cities, our troubled public schools look to major research universities for vision, expertise, management skills, and resources. And higher education is responding. For example, in West Philadelphia today, Penn, the public school district, and the teachers union have formed a unique partnership to build a new University-assisted prekindergarten-through-eighth-grade neighborhood school. It will feature small classes and learning communities, active professional development for teachers, cutting-edge curricula, and other important innovations. It is not a Penn lab school. It is not a charter school. It is a neighborhood public school intended to bolster efforts to enhance the West Philadelphia community. We also intend to build a magnet science and technology public high school near the Penn campus.

Finally, central to all of these efforts and the conversations through which they are instrumentalized is the willing participation of universities and their neighbors in the dialogues of democracy, which are rarely smooth and rarely easy but which are the only way to gain the long-term benefits of mutual trust and understanding and build the strong, inclusive communities we need. We must understand that real progress requires us to ask what we can do *with* the community, not *for* or *to* the community. I am convinced that sustained community partnerships will help define successful universities in the twenty-first century, and such partnerships will fail in the absence of a continuous, honest, and ultimately productive civic dialogue around the shared tasks we can only undertake together.

Concrete efforts such as these—stimulated, deepened, and enhanced by the theoretical understanding and research of our faculty and students— are essential components in the regeneration of older cities, the management of suburban growth, and the reorganization of metropolitan areas to meet the new geographic realities that are among the most complex issues of our time.

At the same time, American colleges and universities cannot fulfill their traditional missions of education and research if they do not learn from the practice and experience of real citizens in real communities. Like Penn, many institutions and individuals have begun to recognize this and are undertaking the continuing research, creative experimentation, and complex public policy discussions that will be needed to frame an effective urban policy agenda for the new century.

It is, then, in this spirit, reflecting the unity of theory and practice that is Penn's unique heritage, that we believe the urban policy agenda for a new century must begin and these contributions to it are offered.

Suggestions for Further Reading

CHAPTER 1: REGIONAL IMPERATIVES OF GLOBAL COMPETITION

America's Choice: High Skills or Low Wages!, The Report of the Commission on the Skills of the American Workforce, National Center on Education and the Economy, Rochester, N.Y., 1990.

Hershberg, Theodore, "The Case for New Standards in Education," *Education Week,* December 10, 1997.

Orfield, Myron, *Metropolitics: A Regional Agenda for Community Stability,* Brookings Institution Press, Washington, D.C., 1997.

Rusk, David, *Inside Game/Outside Game: Winning Strategies for Saving Urban America,* Brookings Institution Press, Washington, D.C., 1999.

CHAPTER 2: PLANNING METROPOLITAN REGIONS

Garreau, Joel, *Edge City, Life on the New Frontier,* Doubleday, New York, 1991.

Garvin, Alexander, *The American City: What Works, What Doesn't,* McGraw-Hill, New York, 1995.

Hall, Peter G., *Urban and Regional Planning,* 3rd Edition, Routledge, New York, 1992.

Nivola, Pietro S., *Laws of the Landscape: How Policies Shape Cities in Europe and America,* Brookings Institution Press, Washington, D.C., 1999.

CHAPTER 3: SOCIAL EQUITY AND METROPOLITAN GROWTH

Beatley, Timothy, and Kristy Manning, *The Ecology of Space,* Island Press, Washington, D.C., 1997.

Bryant, Bunyan, ed., *Environmental Justice: Issues, Policies and Solutions,* Island Press, Washington, D.C, 1995.

Porter, Douglas R., *Managing Growth in America's Communities,* Island Press, Washington, D.C., 1997.

Chapter 4: Regional Design: Local Codes as Cause and Cure of Sprawl

Arendt, Randall, et al., *Charter of the New Urbanism,* McGraw-Hill, New York, 2000.

Barnett, Jonathan, *The Fractured Metropolis: Improving the New City, Restoring the Old City, Reshaping the Region,* HarperCollins, New York, 1995.

Meck, Stuart, et al., *Planning Communities for the Twenty-first Century,* American Planning Association, Chicago, 1999.

Chapter 5: Next Steps in Controlling Pollution

Duane, Timothy, "Environmental Planning Policy in a Post-Rio World," *Berkeley Planning Journal,* Vol. 7, 1992.

Farrell, Alex, and Maureen Hart, "What Does Sustainability Really Mean? The Search for Useful Indicators," *Environment,* Vol. 40, no. 9, 1998.

Raufer, Roger, *Pollution Markets in a Green Country Town,* Praeger, Westport, Conn., 1998.

Chapter 6: Highway Planning and Land Use: Theory and Practice

Beimborn, Edward, Rob Kennedy, and William Schaefer, *Making Transportation Models Work for Livable Communities,* Citizens for a Better Environment, and The Environmental Defense Fund, Washington, D.C., 1996.

Downs, Anthony, *Stuck in Traffic: Coping with Peak-Hour Traffic Congestion,* The Brookings Institution, Washington, D.C., 1992.

Putman, Stephen, *Integrated Urban Models 2: New Research and Applications of Optimization and Dynamics,* Pion Limited, London, 1991.

Transportation Research Board, National Research Council (U.S.), *Expanding Metropolitan Highways: Implications for Air Quality and Energy Use,* Special Report Number 245, Washington, D.C., 1995.

Weiner, Edward, *Urban Transportation Planning in the United States: An Historical Overview,* Praeger, Westport, Conn., 1999.

Chapter 7: Improving Primary and Secondary Education

Lagemann, Ellen Condliffe, and Lee Schulman, eds., *Issues in Education Research: Problems and Possibilities,* San Francisco, Jossey-Bass, July 1999.

McKnight, Curtis C., and William H. Schmidt, "Facing Facts in U.S. Science and Mathematics Education: Where We Stand, Where We Want To Go," *Journal of Science Education and Technology*, Vol.7, no.1, March 1998.

Stigler, James W., and James Hiebert, *The Teaching Gap: Best Ideas from the World's Teachers for Improving Education in the Classroom*, Free Press, New York, 1999.

CHAPTER 8: IMPROVING PUBLIC SAFETY IN CITIES

Crowe, Timothy D., *Crime Prevention through Environmental Design*, Butterworth-Heinemann, Stoneham, Mass., 1991.

Dunham, Roger G., and Geoffrey P. Alpert, *Critical Issues in Policing*, Waveland Press, Prospect Heights, Ill., 1997.

Kelling, George L., and Catherine M. Coles, *Fixing Broken Windows*, Simon and Schuster, New York, 1997.

CHAPTER 9: WELFARE REFORM, REPRODUCTIVE REFORM, OR WORK REFORM?

Center on Budget and Policy Priorities briefs: http://www.cbpp.org.

Gordon, Linda, *Pitied but Not Entitled: Single Mothers and the History of Welfare*, The Free Press, New York, 1994.

Iversen, Roberta R., "TANF Policy Implementation: The Invisible Barrier," *Journal of Sociology and Social Welfare*, June 2000.

CHAPTER 10: HOUSING AND URBAN COMMUNITIES

Burchell, Robert W., and David Listokin, "Influences on United States Housing Policy," *Housing Policy Debate*, Vol. 6, no. 3, 1995.

Green, Richard K., and Stephen Malpezzi, *A Primer on U.S. Housing Markets and Housing Policy*, The Urban Institute, Washington, D.C., 2000.

Joint Center for Housing Studies of Harvard University, *The State of the Nation's Housing*, Harvard University Press, Cambridge, Mass., 1999.

CHAPTER 11: RESTORING NATURAL RESOURCES AND REBUILDING URBAN COMMUNITIES

Jackson, Kenneth, *Crabgrass Frontier: The Suburbanization of the United States*, Oxford University Press, New York, 1985.

Spirn, Anne Whiston, *The Granite Garden: Urban Nature and Human Design*, Basic Books, New York, 1984.

——, "Reclaiming Common Ground: Water, Neighborhoods, and Public Spaces," in *The American Planning Tradition: Culture and Policy*, edited by Robert Fishman, Woodrow Wilson Press and Johns Hopkins University Press, Washington, D.C., and Baltimore, M.D., 2000.

CHAPTER 12: DOWNTOWNS: COMPETITIVE FOR A NEW CENTURY

Houstoun, Lawrence O., *Business Improvement Districts,* Urban Land Institute, Washington, D.C., 1997.

Kotler, Philip, Donald Haider, and Irving Penn, *Marketing Places,* The Free Press, New York, 1993.

Mitchell, Jerry, *Business Improvement Districts and Innovative Service Delivery,* Price-WaterhouseCoopers, 1999.

Whyte, William H., *City: Rediscovering the Center,* Doubleday, New York, 1988.

About the Contributors

JONATHAN BARNETT is the principal of Jonathan Barnett, FAIA, AICP, an urban design and planning firm in Washington, D.C. He is also a professor of the Practice of City and Regional Planning at the University of Pennsylvania. He has been an adviser to many U.S. cities and counties on urban design issues, including long-term consulting relationships with Charleston, South Carolina; Cleveland; Dade County, Florida; Kansas City; Norfolk; Pittsburgh; and Wildwood, a city in suburban St. Louis County. He has also participated in the design of more than twenty neighborhoods and districts in other cities, and in designs for the reuse of former military bases in Philadelphia, San Francisco, Washington, D.C., and Myrtle Beach. He is the author of books and articles about urban design, including *Urban Design as Public Policy* (1974); *The Elusive City* (1986); and *The Fractured Metropolis: Improving the New City, Restoring the Old City, Reshaping the Region* (1995), the latter of which describes the causes of today's fragmented cities and outlines ways these problems can be solved. Jonathan Barnett was formerly professor of architecture and founder of the Graduate Program in Urban Design at the City College of New York and has been the William Henry Bishop Visiting Professor at Yale, the Eschweiler Professor at the University of Wisconsin, the Kea Distinguished Visiting Professor at the University of Maryland, and the Sam Gibbons Eminent Scholar at the University of South Florida.

EUGENIE L. BIRCH is professor and chair of the Department of City and Regional Planning at the University of Pennsylvania, and has been a Fulbright Fellow in Ecuador and a visiting professor at the University of the Witwatersrand (South Africa) and Queens University (Canada). She was a member of the New York City Planning Commission from 1990 through 1995, and the coeditor of the *Journal of the American Planning Association* from 1988 to 1993. From 1995 through 1997 she was the president of the Association of Collegiate Schools of Planning and she was the president of the Society for American City and Regional Planning History from 1986 through 1991. She is the author of *The Unsheltered Woman* (1985) and the associate editor of the *Encyclopedia of New York City.*She is also the editor of the Urban Studies and Planning section of the forthcoming *International Encyclopedia of Social and Behavioral Science.* Long involved in housing, she has published on the history of American housing policy and its present-day application. She is currently working on a nationwide study of the rise of downtown living, funded by the Fannie Mae Foundation, the Lincoln Institute for Land Use Policy, and the University of Pennsylvania.

SUSAN FUHRMAN is the George and Diane Weiss Professor of Education and the dean of the University of Pennsylvania Graduate School of Education. She is also chair of the Management Committee of the Consortium for Policy Research in Education (CPRE). CPRE conducts research on state and local education policies and finance, bringing together the resources of Penn, Harvard, Michigan, Stanford, and the University of Wisconsin–Madison. The Consortium receives significant funding from the Office of Educational Research and Improvement of the U.S. Department of Education. Dr. Fuhrman has written widely on education policy and finance. Among her edited books are *Designing Coherent Education Policy: Improving the System* (1993), and *Rewards and Reform: Creating Educational Incentives That Work* (coedited with Jennifer O'Day, 1996). She serves as co-chair of the National Advisory Panel for the Third International Math and Science Study—Replication and as a member of the Policy Council of the Association for Public Policy Analysis and Management. She also serves on the congressionally mandated Independent Review Panel for Title I. She is a member of the Board of Overseers of the

Center for Education, National Research Council, National Academy of Science and serves on the editorial boards of *Educational Evaluation and Policy Analysis* and *Education Policy*. She also serves as counselor to the Shanghai Municipal Education Commission. Her research interests include state policy design, accountability, deregulation, intergovernmental relationships, and standards-based reform.

GARY HACK is Paley Professor and dean of the Graduate School of Fine Arts of the University of Pennsylvania. He was previously a professor of urban design and head of the Department of Urban Studies and Planning at the Massachusetts Institute of Technology and has taught at other universities in the United States, Canada, China, and Australia. A planning consultant for more than thirty cities in the United States and other countries, his work includes the Plan for the West Side Waterfront in New York City, the redevelopment plan for the Prudential Center in Boston, and the new Metropolitan Plan for Bangkok. He is the coauthor with Kevin Lynch of *Site Planning* (third edition, 1984).

THEODORE HERSHBERG is professor of public policy and history and founder and director of the Center for Greater Philadelphia at the University of Pennsylvania, where he has taught since 1967. In the mid-1980s, he was acting dean of Penn's School of Public and Urban Policy and served as assistant to the mayor (of Philadelphia) for strategic planning and policy development. He holds M.A. and Ph.D. degrees in American history from Stanford University. The center promotes cooperation among governments, school districts, and the private sector in metropolitan Philadelphia, reports on key public policy issues, and functions as a neutral third-party convener. Professor Hershberg's writings appear in *The Regionalist, National Civic Review,* and *The Annals,* and on the opinion pages of many newspapers, especially the *Philadelphia Inquirer.* He lectures nationally on the topics of regional cooperation, the human capital development challenge, and standards-based school reform.

ROBERTA REHNER IVERSEN, is assistant professor and clinician educator at the University of Pennsylvania School of Social Work. Her research focus on occupational attainment among poor women has been reported recently in *Work and Occupations, Social Work,* and the *Journal of Sociology and Social Welfare,* and in an edited volume, *Competence and Character through Life* (University of Chicago Press, 1998). Dr. Iversen is currently examining job retention supports and outcomes among welfare-to-work program participants, staff, and employers in Philadelphia. She is also conducting and directing ethnographic research in Seattle and Milwaukee to examine how attainment of living-wage jobs affects disadvantaged workers, their families, and their communities. The ethnographic study is supported by a grant from the Annie E. Casey Foundation.

JOHN C. KEENE is a professor of city and regional planning at the University of Pennsylvania. Trained in the law (Harvard Law School) and urban planning (the University of Pennsylvania), he specializes in the analysis and evaluation of techniques for managing urban growth, protecting farmland, remediation of brownfields and abandoned industrial properties with potential environmental pollution, and the legal aspects of urban planning generally. As a planning consultant, he has worked with a number of rural counties to develop effective strategies for protecting farmland. He is coauthor of and researcher for two major studies of growth management: *The Growth Management Handbook: The New Jersey Experience* (1989), with Samuel Hamill, and *Guiding Growth: Building Better Communities and Protecting Our Countryside* (1993), with Robert E. Coughlin and Joanne Denworth. He is coauthor of and researcher for two national studies of techniques for protecting farmland: *The Protection of Farmland* (1981), with Robert E. Coughlin, and *Saving American Farmland: What Works* (1997), with Julia Freedgood and Edward Thompson.

PAUL R. LEVY is the executive director of both the Center City District (CCD) and the Central Philadelphia Development Corporation (CPDC). The CCD is a private sector–funded, $10.5 million business improvement district, providing security, crime prevention, hospitality, cleaning, marketing, promotion, and capital improvements for the central business district of Philadelphia. CPDC is a membership organization supported by the downtown business community that conducts research, advocacy, and planning to improve the competitiveness of Center City Philadelphia. Mr. Levy holds a Ph.D. in history from Columbia University and teaches in both the undergraduate Urban Studies Department and the graduate City Planning program at the University of Pennsylvania.

STEPHEN H. PUTMAN, is professor and chairman of the Graduate Group in City and Regional Planning, at the University of Pennsylvania. His teaching and research focus on the use of quantitative methods to understand metropolitan transportation and land use interactions, and on the use of this understanding to assist both in forecasting and in the design and evaluation of regional land use and transportation policies. His writings include the books *Integrated Urban Models 2: New Research and Applications of Optimization and Dynamics* (1991), *Integrated Urban Models: Policy Analysis of Transportation and Land Use* (1983), and numerous journal articles. Putman has spent more than thirty-five years in improving planning practice by incorporation of the practical results from theory development. He has maintained an active role in the application of these techniques, and his consulting firm has an international reputation for integrated transportation and land use model development and application. His transportation and land use modeling software, the use of which is an integral part of his teaching, has been used for forecasting and policy evaluation in sixteen North American cities as well as internationally.

ROGER RAUFER is an independent consulting engineer and an adjunct professor at the University of Pennsylvania, where he teaches courses in urban environmental management. He is the author of two books on environmental topics, *Pollution Markets in a Green Country Town* (1998) and *Acid Rain and Emissions Trading* (1987). He has been a consultant to the U.S. Environmental Protection Agency, the National Commission on Air Quality, and the World Bank, as well as many private industrial firms and utilities. He is currently assisting the United Nations with pollution control in several Chinese cities.

THOMAS M. SEAMON is the vice president for public safety at the University of Pennsylvania. He commands the university's police department and manages the security and safety departments. Previously he was the deputy commissioner of the Philadelphia police department. During his twenty-six-year career he held every rank in the department, serving in patrol, detectives, and training and human resources. Mr. Seamon is a Fulbright

Scholar in United Kingdom Police Studies. He has served as consultant to many law enforcement agencies and educational institutions. He lectures at numerous universities and is a frequent speaker at law enforcement and security conferences.

ANNE WHISTON SPIRN is professor of landscape architecture and regional planning at the Massachusetts Institute of Technology. Until recently she held a similar position at the University of Pennsylvania. She received a B.A. from Radcliffe College and an M.L.A. from the University of Pennsylvania. Her book, *The Granite Garden: Urban Nature and Human Design* (1984),won the President's Award of Excellence from the American Society of Landscape Architects. Her recent book, *The Language of Landscape* (1998), argues that the language of landscape exists with its own grammar and metaphors, and that we imperil ourselves by failing to learn to read and speak this language. Since 1984 she has worked in inner city neighborhoods on the design of community open space and urban landscape plans. She is the director of the West Philadelphia Landscape Project, a community development program that integrates teaching, research, and community service.

Index

Abortion, 136
Accountability, educational, 21, 110–12
Acculturation, 105
Ackoff, Russell, 15
Advertising and downtown improvements, 187–88
AFDC-UP program, 135
African Americans, *see* Race
Agricultural soil, 173–74
Aid to Dependent Children (ADC), 133–34
Aid to Families with Dependent Children (AFDC), 134–36
Air quality and transportation systems, 91–93, 100–101
see also Pollution
Ambient environmental standards, 79–82
see also Pollution
American Academy of Arts and Sciences, 42
American Farmland Trust, 55
American Housing Survey (*AHS*), 152, 153
American Planning Association, 64
American Public Health Association, 153
American Society for Training and Development, 19

America's Choice: High Skill or Low Wages! (Commission on the Skills of the American Workforce), 18, 19
Annenberg School for Communication, 187
Arizona, 57, 98
Asia, 39, 40–41, 44
Assimilation, 105
Association of Bay Area Governments, 43
Atlanta (GA), 99–100
Automobile, dominance of and dependence on the, ix, 52, 59, 61

Bacon, Edmund, 179
Baltimore (MD), 38
Bangkok, 39
Banks and housing issues, 161
Being Digital (Negroponte), 13
Belgium, 79
Billiard-table theory of zoning entitlement, 64, 67
Bistate authorities, 44
Blue-collar workers, 17
Boston (MA):
    floodplains and vacant land, buried, 166, 168

Boston (MA) (*continued*):
  higher education and civic engagement,
    197
  sewer overflows, combined, 169
  stormwater management, 172
Bratton, William, 122
Britain, 78
Brookline (MA), 38
Brownfields remediation, 24, 57–58, 163
Bucks County (PA), 36, 37
Business improvement districts (BIDs),
    183–86, 192

California:
  agricultural soil, 173–74
  air quality and transportation systems,
    91
  entertainment and suburban residential
    clusters, 34–35
  farmland protection, 55
  high-tech communities, 36
  natural resource protection, 57
  policing, 121
  zoning, 44, 73
Cameras and policing, 127
Canada, 40
Capital markets, global, 12–13
Center City District (CCD), 183
Center on Budget and Policy, 144
Central Valley (CA), 55
Charlotte-Mecklenburg Planning
  Commission, 43
Charlottesville (VA), 37
Charter schools, 37, 44, 112–14
Chicago Area Transportation Study
  (CATS), 94, 97–98
Chicago Metropolis 2020, 42
City revitalization, encouraging inner,
    25–28, 37–38, 62
  see also Downtowns; Safety in cities,
    improving public
Civic engagement, the university and,
    195–98
Cleveland (OH), 37–38, 42
Cleveland State Law Review, 77
Clinton, Bill, 109
Colleges and civic engagement, 195–98

Colorado, 170–71
Command and control schools, 18
Command/control regulation, 77–78, 83
Commerce Department, U.S., 63
Commercial Club of Chicago, 42
Commercial strip development, 2–3,
    33–35, 68–69
Commission on the Skills of the American
  Workforce, 18
Communications technology, 13
Community Development Block Grants,
    160
Community policing, 121–22
Community service districts, 44
Community service representatives
  (CSRs), 185–86
Competitive, making downtown more,
    186–88, 192
Core cities, encouraging revitalization of,
    25–28, 62
  see also Downtowns; Safety in cities,
    improving public
County Assistance Offices (CAOs), 140
Crime, xi, 121, 124, 187
  see also Safety in cities, improving
    public
Cultures, similarities between regional, 3
Curriculum, lack of focus/depth in the,
    106
Curriculum, national, 107–10

Dade County (FL), 73
Dallas-Fort Worth (TX), 38, 98
Delaware, 36
Densities found in newly urbanized areas,
  disproportionately low, 59
Denver (CO), 170–71
Design, regional:
  current land-use districts, problems
    with, 68–70
  grading and tree-cutting ordinances,
    67–68
  individual citizens/local governments
    having control over, 63
  land as landscape, recognizing, 64–65
  planned unit development, 65–66
  recommendations, 73–75

subdivision codes, 66–67
zoning, environmental, 67
zoning, improving current, 70–73
zoning positive as well as negative,
    making, 68
Detroit (MI), 25, 174
Development:
    commercial strip, 2–3, 33–35, 68–69
    difficult development areas, 159
    growth contrasted with, 15
    problems with current, 32–35
    scattered-site, 155
    strategies and a permanent mechanism
        for promoting them, 42–44
    see also Growth; Social equity and
        metropolitan growth; Sprawl;
        individual subject headings
Difficult development areas (DDAs), 159
Disinvestment in older urban areas, public
    policies to promote ownership of
    individual homes and, 2
Diversity:
    American society, 105
    neighborhood, 35–36
    regional, 36–38
Donora Valley (PA), 79
Downtowns:
    competitive, making downtown more,
        186–88, 192
    decline of Philadelphia's economy and
        renewal of Center City, 177–79
    financing permanent improvements,
        188–90
    future of traditional, 35
    infrastructure, city, 172–74
    lessons for public policy, 190–91
    perspective, putting downtown renewal
        in, 181
    private sector managing, 183–86
    recommendations, 191–93
    transformation of downtown
        Philadelphia, 179–81
    twenty-first century, repositioning
        downtown for the, 182–83
Dragnet (TV show), 120
Drainageways, 66
Drucker, Peter, 15, 105

Drug problem, strategies for handling the,
    128–29

Earned Income Tax Credit (EITC),
    143–44
East Hampton (NY), 37
Economic regulatory approaches and
    controlling pollution, 83–85
Economy, winner-take-all, 105
Edge Cities, 33–35, 181
Education:
    accountability, 21, 110–12
    American students' school performance
        compared to other nations, 18–19
    charter schools, 37, 44, 112–14
    civic engagement, higher education and,
        195–98
    "command and control" schools, 18
    curriculum, lack of focus/depth in the,
        106
    curriculum standards, 107–10
    governance, 112–14
    investment mentality toward educational
        policy, 118
    mixed-income housing policies, xii
    multifaceted approach to solving
        problems, 116
    performance contracts for teachers and
        administrators, 21
    post-secondary training system for the
        non–college bound, 19
    problems in U.S., 106–8
    reasons for keeping education at the top
        of the national agenda, 105–6
    reforming K–12 education, 19–21,
        27
    respect for, 106–7
    responsibility, who has, 116–18
    socioeconomic status and school
        success, xiii
    suburban-to-urban school comparison,
        18
    teacher quality, 107, 114–15
    teachers, massive retraining of the
        nations', 20–21
    technology favoring the better educated,
        17

Education (*continued*):
  voucher system for school choice,
    112–14
Elastic cities, 41
El Cerrito (CA), 34–35
Employment, mismatch between location
  of jobs and those in need of, 32
End of the Nation State, The: The Rise of
  Regional Economies (Ohmae), 14
Entertainment and suburban residential
  clusters, 34–35
Entertainment aspects of downtown, 182
Environment:
  goal setting, 78–83
  justice, environmental, 52, 59–62
  zoning, environmental, 67, 74
  see also Natural resources and
    rebuilding urban communities
Environmental Protection Agency (EPA):
  brownfield remediation, 58, 163
  Clean Air Act, 93
  compliance with clean air standards, 99
  risk assessment, 81
  sewer overflows, combined, 169
Erodible soils/land formations, 66
Europe, 39, 40, 78
Exports, 12

Fannie Mae, ix–x, 159, 162
Farmland protection, 55–56, 62
Farmland to residential communities,
  conversion of, 24
Farms/forests being lost to new
  development, 2
Federal Bureau of Investigation (FBI), 119
Federal Home Loan Mortgage
  Corporation (Freddie Mac), 159, 162
Federal Housing Administration (FHA),
  ix, x, 51, 151
Federal National Mortgage Association
  (Fannie Mae), ix–x, 159, 162
Federal Reserve Bank of New York, 17
Female-headed households and
  homeownership, 152
Financing downtown improvements,
  188–90
Floodplains and vacant land, buried,
  166–68

Florida:
  entertainment and suburban residential
    clusters, 34–35
  growth management plans, 54
  specialization of metropolitan areas,
    lifestyle-based, 36
  zoning, improving, 73
Forecasting and transportation planners,
  96–100
Forests/farms being lost to new
  development, 2
Franklin, Benjamin, 196
Freddie Mac, 159, 162
Free market determinism, x
Free trade, 12

Garden neighborhoods, 38
Garreau, Joel, 33, 181
Gasoline tax, 61
Gender and work roles, mythic
  construction of proper, 132
Georgetown (DC), 38
Georgia:
  air standards, compliance with clean,
    99–100
  growth management plans, 53, 54
Germany, 127
Ginnie Mae, 159
Giuliani, Rudolph, 122
Global economy, 12–13
  see also Regional imperatives of global
    competition
Global warming, 86
Goods and services, regions and, 14,
  21–23
Gordon, Linda, 132, 133
Governance system, educational,
  112–14
Government:
  bistate authorities, 44
  downtown improvements, 190–91
  fractionated and Balkanized, 52–53
  homeownership, increasing the rates of,
    2, 150–52
  housing programs, targeted federal,
    161–62
  public housing, 153–57, 160–61,
    168

redevelopment programs, federally
    funded housing, 179
regional imperatives of global
    competition, 22–23
rewarding cities that do things well, 192
security enterprises, establishing
    secondary mortgage performance
    goals for government, 159–60, 163
subsidizing exurban growth, 175, 176
see also Local government
Government National Mortgage Authority
    (Ginnie Mae), 159
Grading ordinances, 67–68, 73–74
Grant-in-aid programs for sewerage
    systems, 51
Greenways, 170
Gridlocked streets and highways, 1
Growing Smart Legislative Guidebook
    (American Planning Association), 64
Growth:
    development contrasted with, 15
    management programs, 53–55
    smart, 63, 159
    subsidizing exurban, 175, 176
    see also Development; Social equity and
        metropolitan growth; Sprawl;
        individual subject headings

Habits of mind, 20
Harvard University, 156
Hawaii, 53
Health and Human Services, U.S.
    Department of (HHS), 141, 163
Higher education and civic engagement,
    195–98
Highland Park (TX), 38
High-tech communities, 36, 37
Highways:
    air quality, 91–93
    facilitating growth and development, 50
    forecasts and plans, 96–100
    growth management programs, 54
    historical and political context, 91–94
    linked transportation and land-use
        planning approach, 94–96
    premature obsolescence, 89–90
    problems of modern society, symptoms
        of underlying, 1, 2

recommendations, 101
Hispanic Americans, see Race
Homeless and downtown improvements,
    188
Homeownership, increasing the rates of,
    150–52
    see also Housing issues
Home Owners Loan Corporation, 51
Hong Kong, 39
Hoover, Herbert, 63
HOPE VI program, 160–61, 163, 168
Hospitality industry, 182–83
Housing and Urban Development, U.S.
    Department of (HUD), 149, 153,
    162–63, 168
    see also Housing issues
Housing issues:
    abandoning solid houses, 174–75
    city centers, growing interest in living
        in, 38
    Community Development Block
        Grants, 160
    Community Reinvestment Act of 1977,
        161
    definition of the housing problem, the
        evolving, 149–50
    demand overtaking need, 173–74
    disinvestment in older urban areas,
        public policies to promote
        ownership of individual homes and,
        2
    future, right policies for the, 162–63
    government security enterprises,
        establishing secondary mortgage
        performance goals for, 159–60
    historical look at housing policies,
        150–57
    homeownership, increasing the rates of,
        2, 150–52
    important role played by housing
        industry, 149
    low-income households, 153, 157–58
    Low Income Housing Tax Credit
        (LIHTC), 158–59
    manufactured housing, 155–56
    mixed-income housing policies, xii–xiii
    mix of housing types, encouraging a, 61
    policy planning and funding, 162

Housing issues (*continued*):
  programs for making housing more
      affordable, 158–62
  public housing, 153–57, 160–61,
      168
  quality and affordability, 152–57
  recommendations, 163–64
  redevelopment programs, federally
      funded housing, 179
  redlining, 51
  targeted federal housing programs,
      161–62
  zoning categories, proliferation of,
      69–70
Howard, Ebenezer, 39
Human resources, developing, 16–21

Illinois:
  Chicago Area Transportation Study, 94,
      97–98
  Chicago Metropolis 2020, 42
  garden neighborhoods, 38
  Northeastern Illinois Planning
      Commission, 94, 97–98
Immigrants, 105
Imports, 12
Income distribution/inequality, 17, 105,
      107
Information technology, 13
Infrastructure:
  city, 172–74
  educational, 108
  regional, 14, 32
Inner-ring suburbs, decline of, 23
*Inside-Game, Outside-Game: Winning
    Strategies for Saving Urban America*
    (Rusk), 24
*International Math and Science Study
    (Third)*, 18–19, 106
Internet, the, 13
Investment:
  city administration more friendly to, 191
  educational policy, investment mentality
      toward, 118
  regional imperatives of global
      competition and investment capital,
      23–24

Jakarta, 39
Japan, 39, 40–41, 44
Job Opportunities and Basic Skills (JOBS)
    Training Program, 135
Johnson, Curtis, 14
Joint Center for Housing Studies, 156

Kennan, George, 28–29
Kennedy, John F., 134
Knowledge society, 105

Labor Department, U.S., 141, 142
Labor Statistics, Federal Bureau of, 19
Lake Tahoe, 57
Lancaster (PA), 24
Land as landscape, recognizing,
      64–65
Land-use planning approach, the linked
      transportation and, 94–96
Land values, taxes on increased, 44
Legislation:
  (MD) Economic Growth, Resource
      Protection and Planning Act of
      1992, 55
  (NJ) Land Use Law of 1985, 53
  (OR) Land Use Law of 1973, 53
  (PA) Land Recycling Laws of 1995, 58
  (U.S.) Clean Air Act, 61–62, 93, 100
  (U.S.) Clear Air Act amendments
      (CAAA), 91, 92
  (U.S.) Clean Water Act, 61
  (U.S.) Community Reinvestment Act
      (CRA) of 1977, 161, 164
  (U.S.) Federal-Aid Highway Act of
      1956, ix, x
  (U.S.) Federal Emergency Relief Act
      (FERA) of 1933, 141
  (U.S.) Financial Institutions Reform,
      Recovery and Enforcement Act of
      1989, 161
  (U.S.) Housing Act of 1949, 59–60
  (U.S.) Housing and Community
      Development Act of 1974, 156
  (U.S.) Housing and Urban Renewal Act
      of 1954, 152–53
  (U.S.) Intermodal Surface Transportation
      Efficiency Act (ISTEA), 91, 93, 100

(U.S.) National Environmental Policy Act (NEPA), 94

(U.S.) Personal Responsibility and Work Opportunity Reconciliation Act (PRWORA) of 1996, 136–41

(U.S.) Public Welfare Amendments of 1962, 134

(U.S.) Social Security Act of 1935, 133

(U.S.) Superfund, 57–58

(U.S.) Tenement House Act of 1901, 152

(U.S.) Wagner-Steagall Housing Act of 1937, 154

(U.S.) Workforce Investment Act (WIA) of 1998, 142

Legislation, growth management, 53–54, 61

Legislation, prototype-enabling, 63–64

Lifestyle-based specialization of metropolitan areas, 36–38

Livable communities, 63

Local government:
  design, regional, 63
  efficiency of, improving, 191
  pollution control, 86–87
  power/responsibility devolving to, 44
  social equity and metropolitan growth, 53–55
  see also Design, regional

London, 39, 79

Los Angeles (CA), 44, 121

Loudoun County (VA), 37

Low-income households and housing issues, 153, 157–58

Low Income Housing Tax Credit (LIHTC), 158–59, 162

Maine, 37, 53

Maintenance-of-Effort (MOE) funds, 145–46

Manufactured housing, 155–56

Manufacturing economy, 17, 18, 36, 105

Margin of safety and controlling pollution, 79

Martha's Vineyard Commission, 57

Maryland:
  garden neighborhoods, 38

growth management plans, 53–55

Massachusetts:
  garden neighborhoods, 38
  Martha's Vineyard Commission, 57
  regional diversity, 37
  see also Boston

Mass transit, 33, 41

Medicaid, 144

Medium-density neighborhoods, 37

Megalopolis (Gottmann), 36

Memorization and thinking, 20

Metropolitan planning organization (MPO), 43, 93

Metropolitics (Orfield), 23

Meuse Valley, Belgium, 79

Michigan, 25, 174

Mid-Atlantic states, 52

Middle-class families, xi, xii

Midwest, 52

Milwaukee (WI), 112

Minnesota, 36, 53

Misuse of funds in core cities, 26

Mixed-income housing policies, xii–xiii

Mortgage system, 51, 151

Mother's pensions, 132–33

Moudon, Anne V., 34

Myths and welfare policy, 131–32

Name to new regional realities, giving a, 31–32

National Academy of Science, 18–19, 80, 83

National Commission on Severely Distressed Housing, 154

National Council of Teachers of Mathematics, 108–9

National Education Summit, 20

National Priorities List, 57

Nation-states, decline in relevance of, 14

Natural resource areas, protecting, 57

Natural resources and rebuilding urban communities:
  floodplains and vacant land, buried, 166–68
  rebuilding inner city communities and reducing sprawl, 172–75
  recommendations, 176

Natural resources and rebuilding urban
    communities (*continued*):
  sewer overflows, combined, 168–70
  social/economic and environmental
    issues as separate concerns,
    regarding, 165
  stormwater management, 170–72
Negroponte, Nicholas, 13
Neighborhood diversity, new, 35–36
Neighborhoods, who lives in poor, xii, xiii
New Brunswick (NJ), 36
New England, 52
New Jersey:
  bistate authorities, 44
  growth management programs, 54
  Land Use Law of 1985, 53
  mass transit, 33
  natural resource protections, 57
  Pinelands Commission, 57
  planning metropolitan regions, 42
  regional diversity, 36, 37
  Regional Plan Association, 42
New Standards Project, 19
New York:
  bistate authorities, 44
  Community Development Block
    Grants, 160
  Community Preservation Corporation,
    161
  community service districts, 44
  farmland protection, 55
  Federal Reserve Bank of, 17
  housing issues, 152, 161
  local governments, power/responsibility
    devolving to, 44
  mass transit, 33
  natural resource protections, 57
  planning metropolitan regions, 42
  policing, 122–24
  regional diversity, 37
  Regional Plan Association, 42
  sewer overflows, combined, 169
  State University of, 23
  zoning, improving, 73
1960s and civil disturbances, 120–21
Nixon, Richard M., 156
Northampton (MA), 37

Northeastern Illinois Planning
    Commission (NIPC), 94, 97–98

Oak Park (IL), 38
Obsolescence and highway construction,
    premature, 89–90
Office of Family Assistance, 141, 142
Ohio:
  city centers, growing interest in living
    in, 37–38
  planning metropolitan regions, 42
  voucher system for school choice, 112
1000 Friends of Oregon, 42
Opportunity, myth of, 131–32
Orange County (CA), 173–74
Oregon, 53, 54
Orlando (FL), 36

Paris, 39, 190
Pedagogy, 20
Peirce, Neal, 14
Peirce Reports (Peirce and Johnson), 14
Pennsylvania:
  brownfield remediation, 58
  Department of Public Welfare, 139–40
  farmland protection, 55
  growth management legislation, 53
  inner-ring suburbs, decline of, 24
  neighborhood diversity, 36
  policing, 127
  pollution, 79
  regional diversity, 37
  security, private, 126
  University of, 127, 172, 195
  voucher system for school choice, 113
  see also Philadelphia
Performance contracts for teachers and
    administrators, 21
Petrella, Victor, 14
Pharmaceutical companies and lifestyle-
    based specialization of metropolitan
    areas, 36
Philadelphia (PA):
  abandoning solid houses, 174–75
  accountability, educational, 110
  city centers, growing interest in living
    in, 38

Delaware Valley Reinvestment Fund, 161
floodplains and vacant land, buried, 167–68
garden neighborhoods, 38
higher education and civic engagement, 197
housing issues, 161
inner-ring suburbs, decline of, 24
policing, 126
pollution and risk assessments, 82
population loss, 173
public housing, 155
sewer overflows, combined, 168
specialization of metropolitan areas, lifestyle-based, 36
stabilizing the region's core city, 25–26
stormwater management, 172
Temporary Assistance to Needy Families, 139
see also Downtowns
Phoenix (AZ), 98
Planned unit development, 65–67
Planning metropolitan regions:
countries, new regional strategies in other, 39–41
countries, regional trends in other, 38–39
current development, what's wrong with, 32–33
development strategies and a permanent mechanism for promoting them, 42–44
diversity, new neighborhood, 35–36
diversity, new regional, 36–38
downtowns, the future of traditional, 35
evolution of sprawl into new patterns, 33–35
local governments, power/responsibility devolving to, 44
name to new regional realities, giving a, 31–32
recommendations, 45
successful cities/regions, 45
United States, planning for the new realities in the, 41–44

Policing, see Safety in cities, improving public
Pollution:
command/control regulation, 77–78
economic regulatory approaches, 83–85
future of urban pollution control, 85–87
goals, setting environmental, 78–83
highways, 91–93, 100–101
Population issues:
decline in urban populations, 173
densities found in newly urbanized areas, disproportionately low, 59
nonwhite population, growth of the, 28
rural to urban living, ix
sustainability, 3–4
Port Authority of New York and Jersey, 44
Portland (ME), 37
Poverty:
costs of fixing the social problems in core cities, 26
environmental justice, 59–60
mixed-income housing policies, xii–xiii
push and pull factors, xi–xii
school success, socioeconomic status and, xiii
undesirable facilities placed near minority communities, 52
see also Welfare
Premature obsolescence and highway construction, 89–90
Price-based regulation and controlling pollution, 85
Princeton (NJ), 37
Private sector managing downtowns, 183–86
Private security, 124–26
Problems of modern society, symptoms of underlying:
farms/forests being lost to new development, 2
gridlocked streets and highways, 1
resource disparities, 1–2
subdivision codes, 2–3
zoning, 2–3
Promotion, social, 111–12
Promotions and downtown improvements, 187–88

Property taxes, 56
Public housing, 153–57, 160–61, 168
Pull factors, newer suburbs exerting, xi–xii
Purchase agricultural conservation easements (PACE), 56
Push factors, concentrated poverty and, xi–xii

Quantity-based approach and controlling pollution, 85

Race:
    Aid to Dependent Children, 133–34
    environmental justice, 59–60
    homeownership, 152
    poor neighborhoods, inhabitants of, xii, xiii
    population of nonwhite Americans, growth in, 28
    redlining, 51
    shaping metropolitan areas' evolution over the past five decades, xi
    undesirable facilities placed near minority communities, 52
Real estate, decline in the value of urban, 25
Redevelopment programs, federally funded housing, 179
Redlining, 51
Redundant spending, 23, 24
Regional cultures, similarities between, 3
Regional diversity, new, 36–38
Regional imperatives of global competition:
    cooperation between regions, 11–12
    core city, stabilize the region's, 25–28
    global economy, emergence of the, 12–13
    goods and services, lower the costs of, 21–23
    human resources, developing, 16–21
    investment capital, 23–24
    regional issues, urgency of, 28–29
    regions as basic units of domestic/worldwide competition, 14–16

successful regional cooperation, formulas for, 15–16
    see also Design, regional; Planning metropolitan regions
Regional Plan Association (RPA) of New York and New Jersey, 42
Regional solutions for downtown improvements, 193
Rendell, Ed, 26, 182
Reproductive rights, 136
Research Triangle (NC), 36
Resnick, Lauren, 20
Resource disparities, 1–2
    see also Natural resources and rebuilding urban communities
Retirees, 36
Rhode Island, 53
Ridge, Governor Tom, 113
Risk effect and ambient pollutant concentrations, 80–82
River Oaks (TX), 38
Rochester (MN), 36
Rockefeller Institute of Government, 23
Roland Park (MD), 38
Rusk, David, 41

Safety in cities, improving public:
    community policing, 121–22
    national safety codes, 129
    police procedures, history of, 119–24
    policing, new trends in, 124–27
    professional policing model, 120
    recommendations, 127–29
    team policing, 121
    technology, adapting to new, 126–27
Salaries/benefits and urban reform, 27–28
San Diego Association of Governments, 43
Save the Bay, 42
Scattered-site development, 155
School success and socioeconomic status, xiii
    see also Education
Security, private, 124–26
Services and urban reform, city, 27
Sewage treatment plants, 54
Sewer overflows, combined, 168–70
Sierra Club, 94

Silicon Valley (CA), 36
Simmonds, Roger, 38–39
Singapore, 39
Single mothers, 132–38, 152
Small Business Administration (SBA), 163
Smart Growth, 63, 159
Smog of London in 1952, killer, 79
Smyrna (TN), 36
Social equity and metropolitan growth:
    brownfields remediation, 57–58
    consequences of urban sprawl, 50–53
    costs of fixing the social problems in
        core cities, 26
    densities and automobile primacy,
        disproportionately low, 59
    environmental justice, 59–60
    farmland protection, 55–56
    protecting other natural resource areas,
        57
    questions that must be asked about
        development patterns/growth
        processes, 49–50
    recommendations, 61–62
    state and local polices/programs for
        combating urban sprawl, 53–55
Socioeconomic status and school success,
    xiii
South Carolina, 53
Specialization of metropolitan areas,
    lifestyle-based, 36–38
Sprawl:
    investment capital, unwise use of, 23–24
    natural resources and rebuilding urban
        communities, 172–75
    problems of modern society, symptoms
        of underlying, 2
    shaping metropolitan areas' evolution
        over the past five decades, xi
    see also Development; Growth; Social
        equity and metropolitan growth;
        individual subject headings
State University of New York at Buffalo
    and Albany, 23
Stormwater management, 170–72
Subdivision codes:
    drainageways, 66
    erodible soils/land formations, 66

    land as landscape, recognizing, 64–65
    planned unit development, 66–67
    problems of modern society, symptoms
        of underlying, 2–3
    water-retention requirements, 66
Subsidizing exurban growth, 175, 176
Sustainability, 3–4

Taipei, 39
Taxes:
    automobile transportation costs
        increased through, 61
    brownfield sites, 58
    city revitalization, encouraging inner,
        38, 62
    core cities, shrinking of the tax base for,
        26
    Earned Income Tax Credit, 143–44
    homeownership, increasing the rates of,
        150
    land values, taxes on increased, 44
    Low Income Housing Tax Credit,
        158–59, 162
    problems with current development, 32
    property, 56
    resource disparities, 1, 2
Teacher quality, 107, 114–15
Teachers, massive retraining of the
    nations', 20–21
Team policing, 121
Technology:
    educated, technology favoring the
        better, 17
    high-tech communities, 36, 37
    policing, 126–27
    pollution, controlling, 77
Temporary Assistance to Needy Families
    (TANF), 136–41, 144–46
Test based on standards, national, 109–10
Texas:
    forecasting and transportation planners,
        98
    garden neighborhoods, 38
    voucher system for school choice,
        112–13
Third International Math and Science
    Study, 18–19, 106

Threshold effect and ambient pollutant
    concentrations, 80
Tiebout, Charles, 32
Tokyo, 39–41
Toronto, 40
Trade, free, 12
Transnational companies, 14
Transportation Department, U.S., 94
Transportation networks, regional, 14
    see also Highways
Tree-cutting ordinances, 67–68, 73–74

University and civic engagement, the,
    195–98
University of Pennsylvania, 127, 172, 195
Urban Initiative at the University of
    Pennsylvania, 195
U.S. Census of Income, 17
Utah, 53

Vacant land and buried floodplains,
    166–68
Vermont, 53
Veterans Affairs, Department of (VA), 51
Vietnam War, 121
Virginia, 37, 55
Voucher system for school choice, 112–14

Wages, declining, 17–18
Warming, global, 86
Washington, 53, 55
Washington (DC), 38
Waste water treatment plants, 51
Water-retention requirements, 66
Welfare:
    Aid to Dependent Children, 133–34
    Aid to Families with Dependent
        Children, 134–36
    downtown improvements, 188
    mother's or widow's pensions, 132–33
    myths surrounding, 131–32

Personal Responsibility and Work
    Opportunity Reconciliation Act of
    1996, 136–41
    recommendations, 141–46
    single mothers, 132–38
    Temporary Assistance to Needy
        Families, 136–41, 144–46
West Palm Beach (FL), 34–35
Wharton School's Real Estate Center, 25,
    26
White Americans, *see* Race
Widow's pensions, 132–33
Wilmington (DE), 36
Wilson, William J., 153
Wisconsin, 112, 142
Women in the labor force, entry of, 17
Work and gender roles, mythic
    construction of proper, 132
Workforce development/welfare, 141
Work Incentive Program (WIN), 135
*World Class: Thriving Locally in the
    Global Economy* (Kantor), 22
World Health Organization (WHO), 79

Zoning:
    billiard-table theory of zoning
        entitlement, 64, 67
    environmental, 67, 74
    Hawaii and statewide, 53
    improving current, 70–73
    land as landscape, recognizing, 64
    local governments, power/responsibility
        devolving to, 44
    mix of activities not taken into account
        by zoning categories, 69
    positive as well as negative, making
        zoning, 68
    problems of modern society, symptoms
        of underlying, 2–3
    proliferation of zoning categories, 69–70
    prototype-enabling legislation, 63–64